THE RIGHT TO WORK

BY NELS ANDERSON

Director: Section on Labor Relations
Works Progress Administration

GREENWOOD PRESS, PUBLISHERS
WESTPORT, CONNECTICUT

Library of Congress Cataloging in Publication Data

Anderson, Nels, 1889-
    The right to work.

    Reprint of the 1938 ed. published by Modern Age Books,
New York.
    1. Unemployed--United States.   2. United States--
Public works.   3. Work relief--United States.
I. Title.
HD3885.A65 1973   331.1'37973   70-136835
ISBN 0-8371-5264-X

DESIGNS BY
PHILIP RAGAN

SOCIOGRAPHICS
PHILADELPHIA

COPYRIGHT 1938 BY NELS ANDERSON

Originally published in 1938 by Modern Age Books, Inc., New York

Reprinted in 1973 by Greenwood Press,
a division of Williamhouse-Regency Inc.

Library of Congress Catalogue Card Number 70-136835

ISBN 0-8371-5264-X

Printed in the United States of America

CONTENTS

FOREWORD   1

I. WHAT PRICE DEPRESSION?   3

II. THE FORM WORK RELIEF SHOULD TAKE   14

III. WHO ARE THE UNEMPLOYED?   30

IV. THE WORK THAT IS WAITING   44

V. THE "USEFUL AND NON-COMPETITIVE" BOGEY   58

VI. PAYING THE BILL   70

VII. HOW MUCH UNEMPLOYMENT IS ENOUGH?   82

VIII. A GOOD DAY'S WORK   96

IX. WORK RELIEF AND THE PRESSURE GROUPS   107

X. WORK RELIEF AND THE PROFESSIONAL   122

XI. MANAGEMENT PHASES OF WORK RELIEF   135

FOREWORD

Public work is a way of creating something for public use. It may be a bridge, a school, or any other needed property or service. Normally, the bridge is built so the community will have a bridge, but incidentally it provides work for people.

Public work may also be a way of using or salvaging labor that would otherwise waste in idleness. For administering public work of this kind, a beginning is made with people who need employment. Labor is engaged so that people may earn a living, and a bridge is built incidentally.

This book attempts to discuss some of the essential elements and characteristics of public work to give employment. It is written with a bias in favor of more public employment when and where it is needed. It is written on the assumption that if unemployed labor is not used, it will be lost, and the cost of idleness will return in some other form.

The reader may wish that more had been said here about the public work of states, counties, and municipalities. I realize that these political subdivisions of the United States do spend vast sums of money, but not a great amount of such money is spent for the kind of unemployment relief with which this volume deals.

The reader may be disturbed because more has been said in these pages about the work activities of the Works Progress Administration (WPA) than about other Federal work agencies. There are two reasons for this: (1) I am better acquainted with the work activities of WPA; and (2) during the two years of operation of the Federal Works Program, WPA has provided more than eighty per cent of the jobs made available to relief workers.

Some readers may be disappointed because I have included no "inside" information and no gossip about how the administrative wheels go 'round. I hope that enough has been said to indicate how the Federal unemployment program has operated to this date. I do not have any "inside stuff" to dispense, and I don't know how or where to find it.

It is true that this book was written from the vantage point of a participating observer in the Works Program, but my attention has been fixed mainly on the administrative problems concerning policy and procedure. Considerable illustrative material has been included, but it falls short of being "inside stuff."

This program is too extensive and too widely decentralized for anyone to know all about it. Management responsibility is spread over many places, as it should be for efficient operation. However, with such dispersed authority, no one is ever wholly on the "inside." Those who function at the control center have general administrative responsibility only and general information only. They aid in making policy and allocating funds, but are on the outside with respect to the million minor details involved each day in the operation of work in thousands of communities.

In this summary I have tried to deal with public work as an antidote for idleness. That issue rises above all other issues about public work. It is one of the challenging problems before the nation. It will have to be faced.

For help in preparing this manuscript, I am indebted to Thatcher Winslow of the National Youth Administration, Louis M. Hacker of Columbia University, and to at least a dozen of my fellow workers on the Washington staff of WPA.

I. WHAT PRICE DEPRESSION?

THE PROFESSOR AND THE DEBT

In 1930 a professor of economics in New York City said, "If we stopped relief the unemployed would have to go to work."

There was no federal relief in 1930, or local work relief, and there was little likelihood of any. New York City had its breadlines and soup kitchens, some of them operated by charities, others sponsored by wealthy "angels." Thousands of working-class families were discovering what it meant to be hungry and homeless.

When the professor, advocate of individualism and free competition, was asked what people who could not find jobs should do, he replied, "The law of supply and demand should be permitted to operate. Any man can find a job if he wants it."

For two years the professor watched his theories collapse. His son, a year out of college, had not yet found a job. His unemployed brother-in-law was living with him. The professor did not get an actual salary cut, but his income was reduced by twenty per cent through the loss of two extra classes. He had, finally, to go into debt.

It was then 1932 and the professor had changed his tune. "Something," he insisted, "ought to be done. The government should give business a hand."

The government gave business the Reconstruction Finance Corporation in 1932, but its benefits did not seep through to the unemployed, or even to the professor. He could not get a job for his son, and his unwelcome brother-in-law was still with him.

Two more years passed. By 1934 the federal government was in the business of relief. The professor's son had a small job with a

3

broker, but there was no future in it. And the boy wanted to marry. The brother-in-law had gone away, to wander about the country in search of work. The professor, confused and unhappy, warned, "This country is going hopelessly into debt. We are heading for the rocks."

In 1935 the professor said to a friend in the employ of the government, "My son is bothering me about getting married and leaving home. Do you suppose you could get him a job with one of the emergency agencies in Washington?"

Today the professor of economics is well off. He is teaching two extra classes again, and lecturing to a group of clerks in a brokerage firm on Wall Street. Although he is still in debt, his own budget is better than balanced. He said recently, "When is this country going to stop going into debt? How are we going to pay the bill? Something ought to be done about it."

The professor's case is an interesting one, not for itself alone, but for the fact that it typifies a shift in viewpoint that was shared by large numbers of the American people during the years 1930–1937.

Looking backward it is not hard to see why, in 1930, the professor, like so many people, felt as he did. Other depressions had come and gone and this one, we were assured, would follow the pattern. No one really expected anything from the government.

Public opinion, in fact, had not changed since 1894 when General Jacob Coxey led an unemployed "Army of the Commonwealth" on Washington with the demand for an issue of $500,-000,000 of unredeemable paper money to give the unemployed work improving the nation's roads. President Cleveland informed the "General" that it was not the responsibility of the government to support the people, but of the people to support the government. Coxey and a few of his followers were arrested for walking on the grass of the Capitol lawn.

Few people criticized President Cleveland for his attitude. The panic of 1893–94, though intense, was short-lived, and the return of good times brought work enough for all.

"YOU CAN'T DO THAT TO US!"

Unfortunately, in 1930 and 1931, conditions, instead of improving, grew worse. It has been suggested that had the gravity of the situation been admitted in Washington, and remedial steps taken, the United States might have avoided the abysmal depths of 1932 and early 1933. The fact is, however, the necessary steps were not taken.

The Smoot-Hawley tariff of 1930, the highest in the history of the country, was defended on the ground that it would keep out the products of cheap foreign labor. Actually, as economists had predicted, its real consequence — and a more harmful one at that time could hardly be imagined — was to provoke retaliatory tariff barriers against American exports abroad.

Mr. Hoover's conferences with leading industrialists were similarly fruitless. Hardly had the employers promised the President to uphold wage levels than they raced home to order mass layoffs and wage cuts. It was as though the leaders in Washington were watching flood waters pour over a crumbling dam while they shouted reprovingly, "Stop! Stop! You can't do that to us!"

And meanwhile, for millions of people, misery and starvation had settled down to stay.

Our professor of economics is still worried, now that the misery has been relieved, the starvation checked; he wants to know who is going to foot the bill. The trouble with the professor, and with many others like him, is that they worry too much about the wrong bill. True, in the past few years we have piled up a formidable national debt. But we have incurred it by trying to preserve for millions of our citizens their birthright as Americans — the right to work, the right to live.

There is, however, another unpaid bill about which our professor is singularly unperturbed. Newspapers never refer to it, nor do propagandists of the Right or Left. It will probably never make good campaign material, for the simple reason that it is easier to comprehend what is spent than what is not spent, what is earned than what is lost. This is a bill for which we got nothing in return. It is the cost of idleness enforced on countless numbers of workers.

In computing that cost, we start with 1929. In that year the national income, which is all the income of all the people, was eighty billion dollars. It declined rapidly thereafter, to a low, in 1932, of less than forty billion dollars and it has gradually come back to something in excess of sixty-five billions for 1936. The loss in national income was a loss that all the people shared, but not equally. If we add together the income loss sustained during each of six depression years, including 1936, we get a total loss of over two hundred billion dollars of national income. This is a bill that has yet to be paid. Its very existence, though unrecognized, exercises a greater retarding effect on recovery than any other debt we could have contracted.

An accumulated income loss of two hundred billion dollars represents more money than all the national income for two more prosperous years than 1929. If that huge income loss were equally shared by 120,000,000 people, the burden per person for each of six years would be about $285. Consider what that would mean in increased purchasing power, in better living conditions, for a family of five for six years — or even for one year!

"PAYING FOR DEAD HORSES"

But because the loss of billions of dollars by millions of people is not equally distributed, such averages have little meaning. The rich man may lose millions and still live in luxury. The laborer, on the other hand, may lose his job and in a month be evicted from his tenement home. During those lean years a few people at the top may have added to their wealth, but the millions in the low income brackets were forced to subsist on less than enough or next to nothing. In 1932 more than 15,000,000 jobless workers were walking the streets. No one knows how many others were struggling along with part-time jobs.

Income losses of one year are not wiped out in the next; they accumulate. The losses of several years are not counteracted by an upturn in business. Houses neglected do not repair themselves, nor is the final cost diminished if repairs are delayed. That applies as well to public properties such as roads, parks, and buildings. The eventual repair of a neglected highway or bridge is usually greater if the work is postponed. The same holds for human bodies run down from too little food, too little clothing, or the lack of medical care.

Eventually the cost of neglect to one's body and property must be paid. Whether these losses are public or private, they hang over in unpaid bills. Farmers have a term for such bills for benefits not received. They call them "paying for dead horses."

The billions lost to workers are really losses in work they did not do as well as in benefits denied to others. Add up all the idleness of the unemployed during six depression years and the result is a labor deficiency of no less than 50,000,000 man-years. Not only the workers and their families, but all who might have shared the benefits of their labor, are forced to bear the cost of those 50,000,-000 man-years of wasted labor. That was a bill for "dead horses" amounting to no less than two hundred billion dollars.

It was not, moreover, that throughout 1930 and 1931 Congress and the President were unaware of the downward trend. Leaders in Washington were just as much concerned as the people, but they were also as much divided about what role government should play in recovery. Confronted with so many conflicting opinions, the government did nothing except to echo the pleas of business not to "sell America short." In the course of this "do nothing" policy the bill for dead horses increased by billions of dollars with each passing month.

It was generally agreed, notably in circles far removed from the unemployed, that Americans would never countenance a dole. The traditional independence of the American worker became a favorite theme in editorial and oration. For some, the sanctity of American institutions seemed jeopardized by the mere suggestion that the government assume some responsibility toward the millions whom industry no longer found it profitable to employ. But slowly, inexorably, circumstances forced President Hoover from his non-interference stand.

Fear paralyzed the nation. Those who could, started buying stocks of foodstuffs, precipating rumors of a shortage and an immediate jump in food prices. Monetary and banking fears sent people scurrying to exchange currency and securities for gold. Uncertainty concerning the soundness of insurance companies frightened others into cashing in their policies. Wealthy men kept yachts in drydock, wealthy women left jewels and furs at home, lest their display make them a target for the desperate. Private charities urged almsgiving as insurance against revolution.

Curiously enough, although there was an occasional outburst of rioting, talk of revolution was far more common in the upper income brackets than in the lower. The poor needed all their energies to keep alive, while for the unemployed there was nothing to do but help one another. They shared their poverty in many ways. Evicted families formed shantytown communities ("Hoovervilles") at the outskirts of every large city. Those who still worked gave "rent parties" to save their friends from eviction; they even launched job-giving campaigns. Groups of industrial workers and farmers organized barter outlets, and members of labor unions who had jobs taxed themselves for the benefit of jobless members. Thousands of unemployed "rugged individualists" sold apples at street corners. In these self-help undertakings the "joy of giving" as a motive was supplanted by incentives much more grim.

SAVE BUSINESS!

So critical had the situation become that finally, at the beginning of 1932, Congress approved the Emergency Relief and Reconstruction Act. No law passed under the later Roosevelt Administration has represented a more radical step than did this emergency legislation. It was the first significant reversal of the American doctrine of *laissez faire*.

Under the new Act the Reconstruction Finance Corporation was created for the following purposes:

1. To provide emergency financing facilities for financial institutions;
2. To aid in financing agriculture, commerce, and industry;
3. To purchase preferred stock, capital notes or debentures of banks, trust companies and insurance companies;
4. To make relief loans to states and municipalities.
   Enacted July, 1932, six months after the original Act.

The initial purpose of this legislation was to save business by lending money to industrialists, bankers, and others at the top. The RFC was empowered to make necessary loans in excess of three billion dollars. But not until six months later was provision made for relief loans, and on those a limit of $300,000,000 in all was set. The RFC was primarily federal relief for the tottering financial structure, not for the millions without jobs. Hence states and localities were naturally slow to ask for relief loans. For the six months ending December 31, 1932, only $80,000,000 had been called for, not enough to pay the nation's relief bill for one month.

Yet in spite of the little the RFC did for the jobless, it made an important beginning. It put the non-interference doctrine on the shelf, and it now seems doubtful whether it ever can be taken off. The RFC was created in the hope that loans to business would stimulate employment, but the billions poured into the coffers of private business did not make jobs. The incidence of unemployment, on the contrary, increased.

THE BLUE EAGLE

The Roosevelt Administration assumed office March 4, 1933. On March 31, Congress passed a bill creating the Civilian Conservation Corps, the CCC. The purpose of the CCC was to give work to young men. The standing force of CCC has been a work army of 300,000 to 500,000 youths enrolled for periods of three months or more. They are given some training, which may be called military, but most of their time is spent at work in the national parks and forests.

The CCC, although not popularly viewed as offering relief work, was really the pioneer relief agency of the federal emergency work program. Most of the 2,000,000 boys and young men who passed through the CCC camps during the first four years of operation did come from relief rolls, and most of the money they earned was sent to their families. CCC is now becoming a permanent federal agency.

In May, 1933, the foundation was laid for a real relief program when the Federal Emergency Relief Act of 1933 created the Federal Emergency Relief Administration. The Act authorized FERA to disburse the $500,000,000 of RFC money as "non-reimbursable grants" for relief purposes to the states and communities. No one intended this to be more than a temporary measure to aid the unemployed until they could find regular public work or private jobs in industry.

FERA did not *lend* money to states and cities, but only made grants which were to be matched by state and local funds. Whenever a state filed a petition for funds on the basis of its relief load, the grant when extended was to be conditioned on the state's pledge to appropriate an equal amount or a percentage of the total. Poor states put up very little, while rich states appropriated more; the average for all was about thirty per cent. When granted, the funds became state money and were distributed through the regular state welfare agencies, or through special bodies created for the purpose.

The New Deal relief program, although more realistic, was based, like that of the Old Deal, on the assumption that prosperity would soon return and that the government could drop back into the old tradition of non-interference. Three months or so of positive New Deal effort, it was thought, would lift the economic system out of the depths into which it had sunk during three years of the Old Deal's watchful waiting.

Although Old Deal and New do not differ greatly in fundamental aims, they do differ widely in their formal programs. The New Deal, because it is committed to action, finds itself with each step drifting toward a new concept of the relation of government to business. This difference grows out of another, which concerns the method of administering unemployment relief. The Old Deal doled out money to the corporations and banks at the top of the ailing economic system; the New Deal has circulated it among the unemployed at the bottom.

To illustrate the difference of method, let us look at the $90,-000,000 lent by the RFC to a Chicago bank. What ultimately became of the money nobody knows; the bank had to close its doors. Presumably the money trickled down through the channels of trade. But the same amount of money distributed to the needy unemployed would have been spent at once by two, three, or more million workers for the necessities of life. It would have entered the channels of trade from the bottom, making work and stimulating business at every change of hands.

It was inevitable, from the very nature of those early relief efforts, that the unemployed on public relief rolls should not be treated as workers, but as so much surplus labor in storage. It was not long, however, before it became clear to everyone that direct relief, or the dole, is a wasteful device for maintaining workers in idleness. American workers are not happy idle. They not only fail to maintain the respect of their friends and families, but lose respect for themselves. Thus, from the outset of FERA, the recipients of relief began to look forward to the work program into which FERA was expected to develop.

RECOVERY ALPHABET

According to plans outlined early in 1933, the emergency direct relief program of the New Deal should have terminated in a few months. FERA was the bottom step in the proposed climb to recovery, the means of sustaining a few million unemployed workers until regular public or private jobs could be provided.

The real public work program was made the responsibility of the Federal Administration of Public Works, called PWA. To this new agency, created about the same time as FERA, was entrusted the distribution of three billion dollars for big public works. PWA money was to be made available to states, cities, and communities for bridges, buildings, dams, roads, and similar projects. The money was to be loaned or granted on a matching basis and the state or other public body was required to provide a definite percentage of the funds. The work was to be done by contract, and the projects were to be big ones on which there would be a high materials cost. The idea was to revive the heavy industries.

It was assumed that PWA, by employing two or three million workers on big projects for a period of two years, would create indirect employment for more than six million workers in private industry. The spending of public money would in this way "prime" the pump of business.

PWA, the second step in the climb to recovery, was scheduled to terminate as rapidly as private enterprise, under the guidance of the National Recovery Administration, the NRA, could revive employment. NRA was a control plan for industry, paralleled by the Agricultural Adjustment Administration, or the AAA, which was the control plan for agriculture. NRA and AAA represented an attempt to regulate production and employment in the United States in the interest, not of any one group, but of the people as a whole. Industry, agriculture, and labor were to be partners in the common good.

The experiment was a colossal failure. Industry could not be persuaded to impose rules on itself, nor to keep them when they were imposed. Powerful farming interests resisted the best efforts of the government to protect the farmers as a whole. The fight against NRA and AAA was finally carried to the Supreme Court where both were declared unconstitutional.

And now, after more than four years, PWA seems destined, too, to pass out of existence, despite two extensions of life beyond its original termination date. PWA did not provide the millions of jobs expected of it. The obstacles to getting off to a quick start were too many. The emergency relief program had to be extended month after month for two years, always in the expectation that it would be discontinued next month or the next.

During that two-year period, FERA had to do what NRA and AAA had failed to do, and what PWA could not do; it had to provide four to five million families with subsistence and some work. Upon this tail-end agency of the recovery program, therefore, fell the responsibility for learning to employ the unemployed rejected by industry.

II. THE FORM WORK RELIEF
SHOULD TAKE

FORCE ACCOUNT OR CONTRACT

With the growth of FERA there came to the fore a much debated issue: What form should public relief work take?

The federal government, like state and local governments, has heretofore always done public work by contract. If the government planned to build a bridge it prepared the plans and specifications on the basis of which contractors were asked to bid for the work. The contract was usually given to the low bidder who then employed the labor and bought the materials.

It was, accordingly, on the contract method that federal public work was to have been carried on under PWA; and if everyone involved in these contractual arrangements had cooperated, if there had been no legal or financial obstacles, PWA might have accomplished what it set out to do. Because it failed of its purpose, FERA, with no work responsibility, had to assume the task of giving work to the unemployed outside the contract system.

Since FERA was not intended to be a work agency in any large sense it had to become one in a lesser sense by doing odds and ends of public work, anything to keep the workers busy. In the beginning much of this work was uneconomical; it was bound to be. Some critics called it leaf-raking. Later it became "boondoggling."

The original plan for public works under PWA was to have the government finance on a matching basis a number of big projects in the states and localities. Big projects would require some direct labor but more indirect labor. For example, let us suppose that a city submitted a project for building a new million-dollar court-house, and that it was prepared to finance the project to the extent of approximately fifty per cent. About a third of all the money spent would go for direct labor on the site. The other two-thirds would be spent for materials. The fabrication and transportation of these materials would require the labor of a large number of workers in the steel, cement, lumber, brick, and heavy machinery industries. It is an ideal type of public work if plenty of money is available and enough projects can be undertaken.

Contractors and industrialists naturally favor this form of public work. Unfortunately for the unemployed, however, the PWA type of project did not expand fast enough and did not employ the kind of labor that was available on the relief rolls. Nor did it serve the needs of other millions of jobless workers including women, young inexperienced workers, and older workers.

Meanwhile, FERA went ahead with its program during the summer months of 1933. By the autumn PWA had fallen so far short of expectations that labor unions and other interested groups presented a new plan to carry on for a few more months. This time it was as a strictly emergency agency that the Civil Works Administration was launched late in October, 1933.

The following were CWA's essential features:

1. Four million unemployed persons were to be given jobs on ten temporary projects, and for this purpose $400,000,000 was appropriated from the funds of PWA.

2. CWA was made an adjunct of the FERA program, but it was operated under the rules of PWA with respect to wages and conditions of work.

3. The workers assigned to CWA projects were taken from relief rolls and from the open labor market.

4. As rapidly as PWA projects could be initiated and put into operation the workers on CWA projects would be transferred to them. This meant that CWA was intended to be a labor reservoir for PWA. It also meant that the projects of CWA were to be of such a kind that they could be terminated at any time as workers were transferred to PWA.

In less than a month CWA found enough temporary projects to employ about 4,000,000 workers. This was a record-making achievement. Thousands of local communities joined in the venture with a degree of zeal and integrity never before known in this country. For the first time in four years of depression, workers had jobs and money.

CWA could not use the contract method because the projects were small and their duration too uncertain. Instead of letting out the work by contract, CWA used the "force account" method, by which the government acts as planner, as supervisor of the work, as purchaser of materials, and as paymaster.

Still the hoped-for transfers to PWA jobs did not materialize. CWA had to have an extension of life, and only a special appropriation from Congress enabled it to continue. CWA was discontinued on March 31, 1934.

A NEW FERA

To carry on with some emergency relief employment, a Work Division was added to FERA. The new division combined the work function of CWA with the relief function of FERA, so that the brief experience of CWA was thus absorbed by the Work Division. The operating units of CWA were taken over as well. These formed the beginning of a new type of work relief.

The new FERA program operated essentially as follows:

1. Federal grants, as before, were made to the states, where they were distributed as state money through the regular or emergency welfare bodies. New FERA money was granted with the understanding that as much as possible would be spent for useful public work.

2. As before, the federal government maintained through FERA an advisory control over the program in states and localities. The government established rules for the selection of workers, for planning work projects, and for determining working conditions.

3. As before, applicants for relief were investigated to determine extent of need. For each certified worker, according to his need, a "budgetary deficiency" was allowed indicating the amount of money he should receive each month.

4. Workers certified as in need of relief were assigned to projects to perform an amount of work each month at the prevailing rates of pay in order to equal their budgetary deficiencies.

FERA thus became a monthly program in the larger framework of relief. In localities where the monthly budgets were low, down to $15 or less per month, it was difficult to schedule many workers for projects. Even if the monthly budget of a worker was $20 and the prevailing rate for his skill a dollar an hour, he could only be scheduled for twenty hours per month. The combination of low budgets and high wages in some places, added to the difficulty of getting local contributions for materials, kept many relief clients from being assigned at all. In the entire United States no more than forty-seven per cent of the "reliefers" were assigned under the new program to work.

From the outset the federal government made every effort to improve relief standards. When FERA began, allowances were as low as $5 per month in some states, and in excess of $50 in other states. In May, 1933, the average monthly relief allowance per family in the United States was about $15. When WPA replaced FERA in July, 1935, the average family relief budget had risen to $35 per month.

In spite of limitations, the Work Division of FERA did an astonishing amount of useful work, enough to convince Congress that much of the rejected labor of the jobless could be salvaged. However, the Work Division suffered from the tendency in some communities to unload on FERA many persons who were not strictly victims of the depression. They were the chronic poor, including many types of persons who have always been the legitimate charge of the local welfare agencies. Once the rolls were loaded down with these unemployables, the able-bodied unemployed found it almost impossible to get FERA assignments.

WPA IS BORN

If the FERA, which ended after twenty-six months, did nothing else, it enabled the federal government to learn something about work relief, and revealed some of the difficulties attending any relief program. Out of that experience grew the more comprehensive "Works Program," established by Executive Order April 8, 1935.

Before discussing the import and objectives of the Works Program, it would be well to consider the experimental aspects of federal relief and work relief prior to the actual introduction of the new program on July 1, 1935.

There was, first, no experience in American history upon which to build a federal work relief program.

Such a program called for new relationships between states and the federal government as well as between states and local communities. It was necessary for the government to establish and maintain high and uniform standards, while at the same time respecting as much as possible the traditional rights of states and local communities. An emergency program destined to go out of existence at any time could not assume too much control in localities.

The federal government had to avoid becoming involved in the purchase of property, equipment, or anything else that might hinder a speedy termination of the program, should there no longer be any need for it. To be useful, without becoming too entrenched, the relief program had to maintain itself within the limits of maximum adaptability.

An even more serious handicap was the fact that to carry on such a nationwide relief program the country had no body of experienced administrative workers. The personnel recruited to administer relief and work relief came from many walks of life. It is significant that so many people of such varied backgrounds could be brought together to produce so quickly the results achieved. It is also significant that with a hundred thousand or more inexperienced minor administrative officials supervising the work in thousands of communities there was a minimum of lost motion and waste. Although billions were spent on the CWA and FERA programs, graft and scandal were conspicuously absent. The remarkable success of the whole experiment is a tribute to the good sense and integrity of rank and file Americans.

Of all the money allocated for relief, almost every dollar got into the pockets of the unemployed, who spent it as it was intended. This is a fact that cannot be brushed aside by those who found fault with FERA and who now find fault with WPA.

The Works Program, which is still in force, had as its general objective to "provide relief, work relief, and to increase employment by providing useful projects."

The following were the basic principles under which the Works Program was established:

1. The projects shall be useful.
2. Projects shall be of such a nature that a considerable proportion of the money spent will go into wages and labor.
3. Projects will be sought which promise ultimate return to the federal Treasury of a considerable proportion of the cost.
4. Funds allotted for each project should be actually and promptly spent and not held over until later years.
5. In all cases projects must be of a character to give employment to those on the relief rolls.
6. Projects will be allocated to localities or relief areas in relation to the number of persons on relief rolls in those areas.
7. The program must move, from the relief rolls to work on such projects or in private employment, the maximum number of persons in the shortest possible time.

In these seven principles lies the philosophy of emergency federal work relief. It must be useful work, with the greatest possible portion of the cost going to labor. It must be self-liquidating, if possible, and quick-spending, so that the workers can get the money with which to buy necessities and thereby keep other workers employed.

These, then, were the major objectives at the start of the Works Program; to do non-competitive work if possible, to employ relief workers at their own kind of work.

Implied also in these seven principles is the government's recognition of the doctrine that the American way of getting a living is through private enterprise, and that it is to private employment that workers should turn as soon as possible.

THE "HOW" OF WPA

Unfortunately, although the Works Program has been in operation now for three years, the degree of recovery that had been hoped for has not been realized. Just as PWA was too slow in employing relief workers on large-scale projects, so private industry has made little or no effort to absorb the unemployed and thus render the Works Program unnecessary.

The method of administering relief under the Works Program has been as follows:

1. Ninety per cent or more of the workers accepted for employment are taken from the public relief rolls in the communities where the projects are located.
2. At first the workers received a security monthly wage as common laborers, intermediate workers, skilled workers, or technical and professional workers. These monthly rates were adjusted to prevailing local wage and relief conditions and ranged at first from $19 for common labor in rural southern counties to $55 in large cities of the north, with a national average of $50 per month. In a similar way the security earnings varied for other work classifications.
3. Workers given employment on the program are assigned by the states and by local public bodies from relief rolls through the United States Employment Service to the projects of WPA. If called for, such workers may be transferred from WPA, which thus operates as a labor pool. Workers assigned to such agencies as PWA become the employees of contractors and are not subject to security wage regulations.
4. WPA is the responsible regulating agency of the Works Program. Its responsibility relates to keeping the funds, examining and passing on proposed projects, determining the number of workers to be employed in states and localities, and writing regulations concerning wages, hours, and conditions of labor for all agencies using relief money.

On WPA since July, 1935, there have been many adjustments in the monthly wage scale, most of them upward. The lower scales under $21 were abolished.

Originally, all workers were expected to do a monthly minimum of 140 hours of work. Today a worker is paid his monthly amount, but he works it out at the prevailing hourly wage for his occupation. Instead of a uniform 140 hours for everyone, the work month varies, according to occupation and hourly rate, from 43 hours to 140.

The month of greatest employment for the Works Program was February, 1936, when the distribution of workers from relief was as follows:

In all agencies of the federal government.............. 3,836,087
Workers on WPA................................. 3,035,852
Workers on CCC.................................. 459,461
All other federal agencies........................... 340,774

The figure of 3,836,087 workers does not reveal the full extent of federal relief. Although FERA was supposed to have ceased functioning July 1, 1935, it really continued for a few months to give relief and to operate some projects. Transient camps, for example, continued for several months. Including single persons and family cases, FERA in February, 1936 was still aiding 2,130,000 persons. PWA, included among the "other Federal agencies," was giving employment to 41,259 workers, solely on projects receiving relief funds. Many PWA projects then in operation were being financed from the original grant of three billion dollars. All workers on PWA in February numbered 155,000.

The WPA portion of the work relief load in February, 1936, was about seventy-nine per cent of the total load. At that time more than half the funds, or nearly sixty per cent, had been allocated to the programs of other federal agencies, all operating at a man-year cost of from $1,600 to $3,000. The month-to-month proportion of WPA workers has been from seventy per cent to eighty per cent of all workers on the program, at a man-year cost ranging from $500 to $800.

These figures for WPA, FERA, and PWA as of February, 1936, indicate that no less than 6,000,000 families and individuals were receiving federal work or relief benefits. If the same benefits were available today, the number of cases on federal rolls would not be less than 4,000,000. Most of those included as of February, 1936, were engaged on work relief force account projects.

THE "BOONDOGGLE"

We have not heard the last of the fight for big projects done on contract. Since federal relief began in 1933 the issue has come up with each appropriation bill. Contractors, industrialists, equipment dealers, and trade unionists have all cooperated in drives to get more money for contract projects and less for work relief. Specifically, they wanted certain amounts of the relief appropriation earmarked for projects of a special type.

Usually when the drive for big projects was on, the newspapers joined the heavy industries in the fight. During the past year PWA has become the symbol of the big contract type of project and WPA the symbol for what is called the "boondoggle," or force account project. In cartoons WPA is pictured with plenty of money to spend, building dog houses, while PWA is shown trying to erect big buildings with inadequate funds.

The ideal situation would be one in which there were funds enough to employ all the jobless on both types of project. There could be more contract jobs if there were more money available for materials. The following figures illustrate how WPA and PWA differ in expenditures for labor and materials:

	PWA	WPA
Cost to employ one worker one year.............	$2,260	$800
Materials and equipment....................	1,280	65
Wages (one year).........................	741	684
Other expenses............................	239	87

PWA in April, 1937, reported 117,201 workers on all projects and of these 24,136, or 19.7 per cent, were from the relief rolls.

WPA for the same month reported 2,085,329 workers, of whom ninety-six per cent were from the relief rolls.

On the basis of work already accomplished by PWA and WPA, it is possible to estimate the way each of these agencies would spend a million dollars on work projects.

	PWA	WPA
Number of workers who would receive employ-ment one year from $1,000,000..............	442	1,540
Number of workers who would be taken from the relief rolls...........................	88	1,478
Amount of money from $1,000,000 that would go into pockets of workers.................	$328,000	$820,000
Amount of money from $1,000,000 that would be spent for materials.....................	$566,000	$ 81,000

On the last item in the above table rests the argument between the defenders of big public jobs by contract and the defenders of the WPA type of public work. PWA and its defenders claim that each work day on the site of a construction project is productive of two and a half days of "indirect" labor. Thus if PWA provides a million days of labor on a housing project, 2,500,000 days of indirect labor should be required to produce and deliver the necessary materials to the site of the job.

The estimate is probably high, but if it is true of a million dollars spent for building materials, would it not be just as true for a million dollars paid to the unemployed and spent for consumer goods which have to be produced and delivered?

The first task of the federal relief program is to get the maximum amount of money to the largest number of jobless workers as directly and quickly as possible. They do not save any of it. WPA workers have been spending for consumer goods from twenty to thirty million dollars a week. It is hardly necessary to point out what effect that has on the nation's business.

To put billions of dollars into the pockets of the needy and to get useful work in return is to open all the stores and factories in the country. Not to put money into their pockets is to leave merchandise unsold on the shelves. That, in effect, is what is happening at this moment because all too few of the unemployed have enough work to live by. Spending for anything save the barest essentials is out of the question.

If the normal processes of business cannot or will not employ these millions of workers the government must put them to work by the most direct method possible, and that is the force account, which represents a new economic relationship between the government and the people.

WORK VS. IDLENESS

More will be said in another chapter about the cost of the work relief program. The bill is no small matter, but very little can be said about it in this discussion beyond pointing out that if this cost were not assumed we would have to face a greater cost in material and human losses.

In general deficiencies, owing to income loss, the American people are behind no less than two hundred billion dollars, most of which accumulated during the early years of the depression when there was no unemployment relief. The figures that follow are trivial compared with the losses that were sustained from 1929 to 1933. These cost figures are approximate for the emergency agencies through 1936.

FERA	$2,946,536,000	for 26 months
CWA	844,067,000	" 8 "
PWA	1,444,727,000	" 40 "
CCC	1,391,640,000	" 42 "
Resettlement Administration	137,695,000	" 17 "
WPA	2,324,258,000	" 17 "
Total for the emergency work agencies.	$9,088,923,000	
Amount spent by non-emergency agencies.	1,578,474,000	
Total federal relief and work funds.	$10,667,397,000	

It should be kept in mind that these figures extend only through 1936.

Herewith we add to the federal expenditures the reported contributions by states and localities:

Federal funds expended through FERA, CWA,
PWA, and WPA, 1933 through 1936............ $10,667,397,000
State and local funds, same period................ 2,940,165,000
Total federal, states, and local expenditures... $13,607,562,000

In 1933, states and communities contributed only $338,793,000 compared with contributions of $1,244,927,000 in 1936. This may show either a greater willingness to share the cost of work and relief or a greater ability to bear the cost.

Federal expenditures, which in 1933 were $1,136,964,000, jumped to $3,853,147,000 in 1936. This does not necessarily mean that more money was appropriated. It probably means that money appropriated for work in previous years was not expended until 1936. These figures, however, mean very little unless they are compared with others. For example, consider the total expenditures figure, $13,607,562,000. It is about one-third the income loss of 1932. For the forty billion dollar income loss of that year we got nothing but "dead horses"; for the billions expended on work relief the country has received countless tangible and much-needed improvements.

Set the costs of relief or work relief against the costs of an equal number of man-years of idleness, and the verdict must be in favor of the work. To deny the unemployed the right to work is to deprive the whole nation of the products of their labor.

THE FOLKWAYS OF PRIVATE ENTERPRISE

INDUSTRIAL SITUATION IN 1929

Overproduction of goods
Stores overstocked with goods
Factories are ordered closed

THE LONG IDLE YEARS BEGIN: 1930

The factories remain closed
Jobless workers have no money
Goods remain on the shelves

Spinning one of the cables on the Tri-Boro Bridge in New York City. Into this monumental structure went $44,000,000 of WPA money. It is a good example of the "big job" kind of public work from which relief workers get very few benefits, even indirectly.

Eastern newspapers made fun of the "Castle for Monkeys" at Little Rock, Arkansas, calling it a WPA "boondoggle." This zoo was designed by a local architect and built out of native red stone with relief labor. Businessmen of Little Rock contributed the collection of monkeys.

Amphitheatre and band shell in the Zoological Park, Toledo, Ohio. A good example of a useful project at low cost. The stone from which the band shell was constructed had previously been removed from an old canal. Ninety-six outdoor recreational structures have been erected by WPA with relief labor in two years.

Farm-to-market road built by WPA along Knob Creek, Tennessee. A southern gentleman said, "If WPA keeps going we will soon have the Civil War paid for." Throughout the United States CWA, FERA, and WPA have built or improved 300,000 miles of rural roads.

Redecking the boardwalk at Ocean City, New Jersey. No resort town along the Atlantic Coast from New York to Florida is happy without its boardwalk. Of these socially popular promenades, relief labor has built or improved many miles.

Laying lateral drains along the Henry Hudson Drive on the New Jersey side of the Palisades Interstate Park. Stone drains are as enduring as cement ones, and cheaper. WPA has laid such drains for 5,300 miles of road.

Operating a roller at the Bolling Field Airport, Washington, D. C. On this project Army officers have demonstrated that relief labor is as efficient as any other type.

WPA park improvement in Providence, Rhode Island. The Federal program has built or improved 6,300 small parks, playgrounds, athletic fields, and golf courses.

Spreading black surface runways for a Philadelphia
airport. WPA has built and improved 215 airports
and landing fields, and built or improved 1,090,000
feet of runways. For the safety of air commerce
8,400 air markers and beacons have been installed.

WPA sewer project at Chester, Pennsylvania. In two years WPA dug or improved 7,200 miles of sewers, built 350 disposal plants and incinerators, 3,500 septic tanks, 780,000 sanitary toilets, several thousand miles of mosquito control and drainage ditches.

A country school in Kansas. In rural areas CWA, FERA, and WPA have built several thousand small schools and reconditioned many more. In one state four hundred schools of adobe or stone were erected. WPA has virtually revived the use of stone for small buildings.

High school at Van Nuys, California. A shockproof
building to replace one that was destroyed by the
1933 earthquake. PWA allocated $470,000,000
for large school buildings.

Easter services of the Federal Music Project at the Hollywood Bowl, California. In such public places WPA has entertained in two years an aggregate audience of 64,000,000 persons. Besides choral groups and dance orchestras, WPA has maintained 48 symphony orchestras, 110 concert orchestras, and 80 bands.

A people's forum in Seattle. The Office of Education of the Department of the Interior has conducted experimental forums in 19 centers where 8,900 meetings were held with an aggregate attendance of 478,000. This same program sponsored 3,200 radio forums and discussions.

A rugweaving project at Greensboro, North Carolina. The labor of women cannot be used to make
roads or build bridges, but it can be employed in
the production of clothing or home furnishings. Of
all WPA workers, 15 percent are women. No other
Federal work agency has any program for using the
labor of jobless women.

Unemployed women repairing books in Greensboro, North Carolina. More than 12,000,000 books have been repaired or rebound in 15,000 public schools, and in 1,800 libraries more than 17,000,000 books have been reconditioned. By this use of relief labor WPA has saved the taxpayers millions of dollars.

THE LONG IDLE YEARS DRAG ON: 1930–1933

Still the factories are closed
Still the workers have no money
The stores cannot sell goods
The workers are dispossessed

AFTER THREE YEARS OF IDLENESS: 1933

Alarming increase of unemployment
Workers move to shanty homes
Goods still remain on the shelves
Industry is hopelessly dormant

THE GOVERNMENT LENDS A HELPING HAND: 1931

The industrialists ask for help
Industry gets federal money
Factories are slow to open
Goods still remain on the shelves

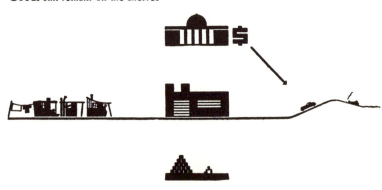

FEDERAL LOANS GO INTO ACTION: 1931–1933

Some factories are opened
Technological improvements follow
Fewer workers make more goods
Unemployment is not relieved
More and more goods pile up

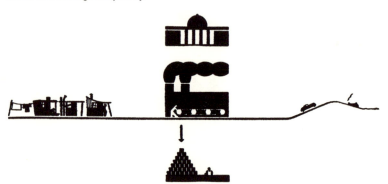

NEW DEAL SPENDING PROGRAM BEGINS: 1933

Federal money is spent for relief
A federal work program begins
Industrialists are encouraged
The workers have money to spend

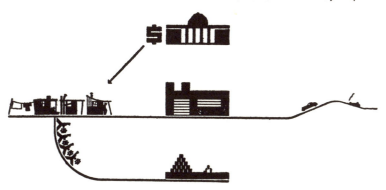

NEW DEAL SPENDING PROVES PRACTICAL: 1934–1936

Workers can buy goods
Stores can buy new supplies
Workers can evacuate the shanties
Factories begin to operate

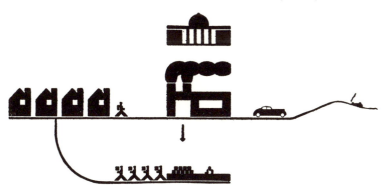

III. WHO ARE THE UNEMPLOYED?

GOD'S REWARDS AND PUNISHMENTS

In 1840, Francis Wayland, president of Brown University, published a college textbook on political economy. Of the virtues of work, he said: "If God have set before us sufficient rewards to stimulate us to labor; and if He have attached to idleness correspondent punishments, it is manifest that the intention of this constitution will not be accomplished, unless both of these classes of motives are allowed to operate upon man."

Such a statement of principle is important because it comes from a book that was used in colleges for a generation, a book that helped develop the American philosophy of individualism.

Nearly a century has passed since Wayland wrote about God's reward for work and His punishment for idleness. He conceded that private enterprise might stagnate, but he said not a word in his book about unemployment. He didn't need to, for there was little in a frontier country in 1840.

Americans of certain classes still cling to the precepts of those days. They recognize but two kinds of poverty — the poverty that results from a man's being too sick to work, and the poverty that results from a man's being too lazy to work. For the sick, the answer was charity; for the lazy, punishment.

There was no place in that philosophy for the idea that poverty may also be due to a man's inability to find work. Wayland would have said in 1940: "Let the idle bestir themselves and find work or let them suffer the fruits of indolence."

Prominent persons who today hold views like these, views that were socially sound in 1840, would balk at using the transportation system of 1840. Yet they are unwilling to face the unemployment situation of 1938 with the same degree of realism that they apply to other current problems. They prefer to deal with unemployment as if enforced idleness were a matter of moral turpitude.

It is true that some men are idle because they are sick and others because they are lazy, but after they have all been crossed off the list we still have millions to account for who are neither sick nor lazy. These unemployed workers represent an economic challenge that is not resolved by moral shibboleths about the discipline of poverty.

Why, if they are able and willing to work, are these people jobless? Who are they, and how great is their number? These are the questions that we shall try to answer in this chapter.

HOW MANY?

The volume of unemployment at any given time is a subject as controversial as the proposals for dealing with it. And since the economic fortunes of all people are in some way involved, any opinions about unemployment are bound to be tempered by the wishes and interests of those who comment on it. That is evidenced in the exaggerated estimates of the volume of unemployment made from time to time by different observers.

Here, for example, are three estimates made about June, 1936:

American Federation of Labor	11,100,000
National Industrial Conference Board	9,700,000
The New York Sun, less than	4,000,000

For the same month the United States Employment Service reported that there were in its active files the names of 6,500,000 job seekers. The total number of unemployed was still greater, of course, because all the jobless do not register with the USES.

Controversy over the country's relief needs became so intense that soon after the Presidential election of 1936 there developed widespread agitation for a census of the unemployed. The "agitators" this time were not radicals, but right-wing politicians, industrialists and bankers. Their slogan was, "Too many people are getting relief. Let us get the facts and stop this political racket." Simultaneously they began renewing the old cry for a balanced budget and lower taxes.

Finally, to put an end to wild surmise and pointless debate, Congress in August, 1937, authorized the President to make a count of the unemployed, leaving to him the responsibility for finding the simplest, quickest, and most reliable method of procedure. With John D. Biggers, a manufacturer of glass products, as administrator, the poll was conducted with the cooperation of the Post Office Department.

Prior to the count, which was taken between November 15 and November 20, 1937, the government launched an extensive publicity and instruction campaign. Registration cards were delivered by letter carriers to every household in the land, and the unemployed were asked to fill out the cards and return them through the postal system.

The initial, over-all returns of the census were reported to the President on January 1, 1938. The totals included two groups of jobless workers, as follows:

Those employed on emergency work (WPA, NYA, CCC).	2,001,877
Male	1,662,444
Female	339,433
Others totally unemployed, able and wanting work	5,821,035
Male	4,163,769
Female	1,657,266
Total emergency workers and other unemployed	7,822,912

In order to determine the extent of the voluntary registration a test census was conducted on November 29 in 1,864 areas in all parts of the country. On each of these carrier routes enumerators made a house-to-house canvass to find out what proportion of the unemployed in each household filled out registration cards. The sample census revealed that seventy-two per cent of the unemployed had filled out the cards distributed for their use.

On the basis of that percentage, it was estimated that the actual number of totally unemployed and partially unemployed persons in the United States, between November 16 and November 20, 1937, was between 7,822,912 and 10,970,000.

To tabulate all the information that may be extracted from nearly 8,000,000 registration cards will take a large staff of experts several months. Two weeks after the total number of registrants was made available on January 1, 1938, the figures were broken down for regions, states, counties, and towns.

THE CENSUS REVEALS . . .

What we now know from the official count is sufficient to silence temporarily those who have estimated the number of jobless at less than 6,000,000 or at less than 4,000,000. Statisticians who have been doing their guessing at the other extreme find that the census tends to confirm their claims, especially since the poll was taken on the eve of the present recession. Between 1,000,000 and 2,000,000 more workers have lost their jobs since the middle of November.

Regardless, however, of whether the census represents more or less than seventy-two per cent of the unemployed, it will yield certain useful items of information about the 7,822,912 unemployed workers reported. For example, we shall learn from it:

1. Where the unemployed are, and what percentage of the employable persons in each state, county, and city are without work.
2. The percentage of Negro and other races, although, unfortunately, the unemployed were not asked to give information about nativity or citizenship.

3. The ages of the unemployed and the number in each state and locality.
4. The number of registrants living on farms or by farming, as well as the number living in towns and cities; also the occupations of those living in urban centers.
5. Data about the training and work experience of the registrants.
6. The amount of employment had the previous year and during the week prior to November 16.
7. The number of other employable persons in their families, and the number of dependents.

When the findings of the unemployment census have been compiled we shall have the information indicated above for all the registered unemployed in any state or community. It will represent an adequate cross-section of the unemployed as reported for November 16 to 20, 1937.

To complete the picture, there should have been, covering the same period, an inventory of job opportunities in private industry for the same states and localities. However, the existence of specified numbers of workers unemployed in different occupations and fields of industry constitutes a negative inventory of employment for such industries. The census will report, for those dates, the number of workers various industries are not using.

Those who are in the best position to know the facts about unemployment will not get from the federal census very much new information. They already know in approximate terms (1) how many unemployed there are; (2) where the unemployed are, in city or country; and (3) what the occupational needs of the unemployed are. Available information at the time of the census was far in excess of the willingness of the government to provide commensurate unemployment relief and public work projects.

There is, however, an important difference between the facts already at hand and the information that will be available as a result of the census. The earlier data related not to all the unemployed, but only to workers who had applied for jobs through the USES, to workers receiving or asking for relief, and to workers on the Federal Works Program. The census will tell us more about workers already receiving public benefits as well as about other unemployed workers who may or may not have been accounted for in previous registrations.

FROM THE RECORDS

The United States Employment Service has made a number of counts of the unemployed whose names are in its active files. These are workers who have asked for jobs and are waiting to be called. Relief workers who get public jobs are expected to register first with the USES. The count as of July, 1936, showed:

6,619,891 — the total number of workers in the active file

5,299,702 of the above number were men, and

1,320,189 of the total were women

3,507,484 of the total number were relief workers waiting to be assigned to jobs in private industry.

It will be seen from these figures that the 6,691,891 workers registered with the USES would be no more than two-thirds of the 10,-000,000 workers unemployed, according to estimates current in July, 1936.

While there were approximately 10,000,000 jobless, of whom nearly 7,000,000 were registered with the official federal placing agency, there were on public jobs for the unemployed about 3,500,000, or about half the number registered with the USES and a third of all the unemployed.

The Works Progress Administration has made its own tabulations of the unemployed, the most comprehensive of which was for March, 1935. This count was also a partial survey, being a report of the unemployed on relief who were eligible and willing to be put to work. This canvass covered:

4,157,813 relief households, in which were

6,151,747 eligible workers, 16 through 64 years of age, of which

4,985,120 or eighty-one per cent had previous work experience.

These counts by two federal agencies prove at least one thing — that in March, 1935, and in July, 1936, more than six million workers were seeking government aid in their search for work. We do not know how many more were seeking work and were not registered with the USES or assigned to WPA. We do not know, either, whether the workers registered with the two agencies were representative of the unemployed. It is probable that they were.

As might be expected, gainful workers are unevenly distributed between city and country. The USES registration for July, 1936, does not show how the applicants were distributed on the basis of urban or rural residence. But the WPA report, when compared with the United States Census of 1930, shows that:

> Of gainful workers in 1930
>> 609 of each 1,000 lived in cities,
>> 391 of each 1,000 lived in rural areas;
> Of workers on relief, March, 1935
>> 653 of each 1,000 lived in cities
>> 347 of each 1,000 lived in rural areas.

The poor of the industrial centers live by nothing save the labor they can sell from one payday to the next; rural workers frequently have other resources to fall back upon. More than any other workers, the unemployed in cities are ill-fed, ill-housed, precariously employed, and poorly protected against hazards to health. They have few, if any, reserves.

It is not surprising, therefore, to find that the large industrial and highly urbanized states head the unemployment list. One-third of all the unemployed reporting for the March, 1935, WPA survey were in New York, Pennsylvania, Ohio, and Illinois. Add to the figure for these four states the workers on relief in Massachusetts and New Jersey and the total for the six leading industrial states becomes 40.8 per cent of the nation's jobless. These six states contained 38.6 per cent of the gainful workers reported in 1930.

The distribution of the unemployed as accounted for by the records of the USES and WPA raises certain other questions which may be answered by the census. Do more people apply for relief in large cities because there is more poverty there, or because relief agencies in cities are more generous and approachable? Some rural communities have no relief at all; but neither do they have a relative share of the nation's wealth. If urban standards were applied, would more people be eligible for relief and work benefits in rural areas than are shown at present on the records of rural public welfare agencies?

UNEMPLOYED WOMEN

The unemployment census reported 7,822,912 persons as totally unemployed, of whom 2,023,098, or about twenty-six per cent, were women.

Jobless women, never a problem in previous depressions, in 1931 and 1932 suddenly made their appearance on breadlines, waiting for food, or at factory gates, waiting for work. Formerly, women and children were expected to remain at home, or to go to the private charities for help. But this time there were too many of them.

When, in due time, job-finding agencies were set up, they usually concentrated on getting work for men. In the same way, such public work programs as there have been were designed solely to assist jobless men.

Today when delegations of the unemployed make demands on city councils or state legislatures, women accompany the men. Women, and even children, take part in demonstrations and parades. In May, 1937, a "Women's Brigade" of the Workers Alliance convened in Washington to demand Congressional approval of the $1,500,000,000 Emergency Relief Appropriation Act of 1937.

That public work has usually conferred the major benefits on men is probably attributable to the fact that most public work calls for manual labor in construction or other outdoor work. But when federal emergency work was initiated the women stepped forward to demand their share of it.

In the two years ended June 30, 1936, the United States Employment Service received 7,585,000 job applications from men and 2,815,000 from women. Of the jobs filled by the USES, 1,323,000 were given to women and 7,631,000 to men. Women comprised twenty-seven per cent of the applicants and got fifteen per cent of the jobs. This is what women received:

Total jobs from the USES............................ 1,323,000
  Jobs on public relief............................... 410,000
  Domestic jobs (more than a month).................. 340,000
  Domestic jobs (less than a month).................. 283,000
  Jobs in factories.................................. 100,000
  Jobs in agriculture................................ 27,000
  Other private jobs................................. 163,000

There is a notion abroad, and it persists, that women with children to support should be content with home relief, no matter how miserably low their budgets. Regardless of her wishes in the matter a widow with small children is urged to stay at home; but a widower with children is expected to get out and hunt for work. It is discrimination of this sort that women are resisting through the various organizations for the unemployed.

In certain states WPA, in reducing the number of workers, has tried to transfer women workers to the rolls of the Social Security Board. Women with children have been forced off the work program and advised to apply for the benefits paid to dependent children. The women's response to that, in Cincinnati, Detroit, and a number of other cities, has been to stage sit-down strikes, protesting such action. To all contrary proposals they have answered, "We don't want to be put on relief. We don't want to apply to the Social Security Board. We don't want old age benefits. We want to work. We have as much right to work as the men."

Usually women workers have met their strongest opposition from local public officials who have not been converted to the idea that unemployed women can do useful work. But they are also opposed by social workers who subscribe to the good old doctrine that women should be at home with their children, and by engineers who would rather plan and supervise projects for men.

These obstacles, however, are probably only temporary, for despite the reluctance of local public bodies to sponsor projects for women there are many more of them than there used to be. In most places, too, the increase has been due largely to the insistence of the women on equal opportunities for work.

HANDICAPS OF AGE AND RACE

Women are actually under no more of a handicap in getting work relief benefits than are the very young or the old. In this respect the work relief program reflects the prejudices of the labor market.

Youth and age seem to be over-represented among the workers on the relief rolls. According to the prevailing practice in public relief agencies, only the "first priority" worker of the family is given a job. Usually the first priority worker is the father, and if he is deemed unemployable, some other priority worker is given the assignment. The other employable members of the family must remain idle.

We do not know how many jobless workers there are among the families of relief recipients. The unemployment census should answer that question. Until it does we have in the reports of the USES some information about the ages of applicants for jobs. Of 10,400,000 such applicants registered with the USES for the two years ended June 30, 1936, about ninety per cent were reported for age. This is how they were distributed:

All USES applicants reported for age	9,374,000	100%
Applicants 20 years and under	1,622,000	17%
21 to 24 years	1,511,000	16%
25 to 44 years	4,092,000	44%
45 years and over	2,149,000	23%

Of these applicants the USES reports 2,200,000 not classified by occupations who are "predominantly persons without recent work experience." Here are the young people "lost between school and industry." Surely, if thirty-three per cent of the applicants for work, including relief clients, are under twenty-five years of age, it is a mistake to conclude that most of the eligibles are old.

If the facts were known we might discover that the relief population is overburdened with inexperienced young workers at one end and at the other with older workers excluded from industry. Closer examination of both the old and young workers would undoubtedly reveal further the extent of the discrimination by industry against these groups.

Motivated by purely profit considerations, private enterprise cannot help but be discriminatory. It is obvious enough that workers are hired, rejected, dismissed, or denied promotion for reasons that have nothing to do with their abilities. It is also clear that basically the racial, political, and other discriminations against them are both socially and economically motivated.

No group of workers suffers more at the hands of discriminatory private enterprise than do Negroes. In many industrial cities Negroes, like the Mexicans, have been brought in by the trainload to replace striking workers, and have then been left stranded. Even in normal times they are the last to be hired and the first to be discharged.

About eleven per cent of all workers in the United States are Negroes and, other things being equal, we should expect to find that they comprised the same percentage of the workers on relief. Instead, we find that Negroes make up fifteen per cent of the relief population. Moreover, only four per cent of all Negroes on relief are skilled workers, as against fourteen per cent of white workers. The percentage of Negroes in cities is also higher than in rural areas.

When disadvantaged groups, including the Negroes, approach federal agencies asking for relief or for public work they should be treated like any other applicants. The fact is, however, that since the federal program for unemployment relief must be administered through communities, it is the local people who supervise the operations and select the recipients of relief in accordance with prevailing local sentiment. And while the federal government can eliminate some discrimination it cannot override the prejudices and traditions of localities, states, and regions.

That the federal program has been fairly free from discrimination with respect to Negroes, is indicated by the higher percentage of colored workers on public projects and relief, compared with the percentage of Negroes in the general population. Jobs are not provided for all Negroes, nor for all white persons on relief, and if in some localities the Negro gets more than a proportionate share of the work, it is due in part to the fact that he suffers more than a proportionate share of the poverty.

MILLIONS OF MAN-YEARS

Unless the information gathered is to be used in remedying the situation, there is no point in counting the unemployed. The first consideration in attempting to solve the problem should be the realization that idleness is costly. We are told that there is a shortage of skilled workers. If such shortage exists, why should not steps be taken to train some of the millions among the unemployed who have never had a chance to acquire skills?

At a time when more trained workers are needed because of the increasing use of machinery, we find that seventy per cent of the relief workers are unskilled, whereas but fifty per cent of the general worker population is unskilled.

This would seem to indicate that the great burden of unemployment is carried by the untrained who work with their hands, if it were not that public work and relief work offer so few opportunities for white collar and professional workers that many of them, in order to get jobs, are forced to classify themselves as unskilled laborers.

Depending on the state, from forty to eighteen per cent of the employables on relief are skilled workers, classified either as workers with industrial skills or as skilled persons that do construction work. The Works Program provides jobs for carpenters and bricklayers but not for machinists or boilermakers. Public work jobs are available for painters, plasterers, and plumbers, but there are few for pressmen, moulders, welders or metal workers. If bakers, miners, tailors, and a million other special or skilled workers are to get any relief jobs, they must be assigned to common labor.

Not to use the industrial craftsmen in accordance with their skills is, of course, to deprive the people of needed services. But to do otherwise would involve the government in a protracted controversy with industry about the production of goods. True, it is better to give the industrially skilled some kind of work rather than none, but it would be a wiser policy to give them their own kind of work. Unable to utilize their skills, WPA has been forced to reclassify such workers to common labor.

From two to four per cent of the employables on relief have had some professional or technical training; they include thousands of teachers, musicians, artists, writers, and actors. These are the most expensively trained workers on the relief rolls, and their continual unemployment, like that of nurses, physicians, and dentists, results in incalculable cultural and social losses. And when professional and technical workers are assigned to common labor, the loss is no less.

Unlike the unemployed in other classifications, the unemployed technical and professional workers also include a higher percentage of women, the ratio being forty per cent of women to sixty per cent of men. Otherwise, except in the industrial crafts, few women are numbered among the skilled workers.

Such information as the government has about the workers on relief has been adequate for an emergency program, but it is not sufficient for large scale planning. The time is not far off when government and industry together will have to review the workers in the hiring line, and classify them according to their capabilities so that there can be in the future a more comprehensive re-employment policy.

There is this to be said for the unemployed, whatever their critics may claim to the contrary: they are people who have worked. In practically all their appeals to the government they ask for work, and what is more, they expect to be provided with work. To the point of despair they have waited for work from private employers. Many of them have lost years of labor opportunity and if, now, some of them seem to have resigned themselves to unemployment, we should not be surprised. The aggregate of all the time that all the unemployed have lost amounts to millions of man-years of good labor of every kind wasted in idleness.

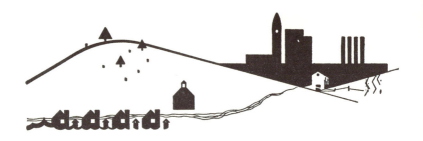

IV. THE WORK THAT IS WAITING

BUYING LABOR TO SAVE IT

A man in North Dakota wrote to WPA headquarters, "In three years I have been idle more than one year, and that's why I'm so far behind. Why can't the government give me work if I can't get private work? There is so much public work to do around here."

From Tennessee a man wrote, "It is not good for us or our town for so many of us to lose work like this. We can't support our families like we want. If the government would hire us there is plenty to be done close by."

A man in Vermont wrote, "I have never been on relief but some of my neighbors have been. They do not get enough work to keep them busy all the time. Then why can't WPA have projects for them to work on when they are idle? My neighbors would rather work than be on relief."

There can be no doubt that the people approve public work, especially relief work, if it is timed and scheduled to meet needs in the seasons of unemployment. When it is not, the result is idleness and loss.

This chapter, however, is not concerned entirely with the losses of labor through idleness. It is an attempt to review some of the fields of public work that await public attention.

Any observing person can find the evidences of labor lost wherever he cares to look. He can detect it in the goods that people do not buy. Unable to work, the unemployed have purchased neither clothing nor household furnishings, and have denied themselves many essentials. Unable to pay for better foods, they are forced to consume cheaper, less nourishing foodstuffs. Pressed for funds, the poor eat bread instead of meat, potatoes instead of the more costly green vegetables and fruit.

Good houses have lost tenants to poorer houses, until slum dwellings everywhere are filled; and despite the obvious need for cheaper and better houses, few are being built. The evidences of labor lost are to be seen on every side in empty stores, vacant office buildings, and idle factories. They can be seen, too, in neglected public property.

Roads, of course, are the most valuable and most extensive of public properties, and so, when federal funds are made available for work relief most localities want to use the labor for road building or for the improvement of roads. Almost invariably a contest develops between those interests that favor expensively paved ribbon highways from which the major benefits go to private enterprise and those that want the less expensive "feeder" side roads, which are not so profitable to private road builders.

Of the 3,000,000 miles of public highways in the United States, some sixty-five per cent were unsurfaced or unimproved in 1935. Even today two out of three farmers still do not have good roads because too much has been spent for cross-country speedways and too little on the side roads, with the result that most rural folk are marooned in bad weather. In the past, road building has received its greatest stimulus from the pressure of city dwellers and automobile interests for hard-surfaced ribbon highways that are used very little by farmers.

The cost of making the necessary improvements on 3,000,000 miles of highways would approximate twelve billion dollars. That sum would allow for:

160,000 miles high type surface.............. $24,000 per mile
840,000 miles low type surface............... 6,300 per mile
2,000,000 miles of dirt road repair............. 1,500 per mile

Consider what the final item — 2,000,000 miles of dirt road repair, mostly on farm-to-market roads — would mean if all these roads were to be so improved that they could be traveled over in stormy weather. In that job alone there are millions of potential man-years of labor.

Street paving, alley improvements, the laying of sidewalks and curbs in towns and cities, would call for work expenditures of from ten to twenty billion dollars.

The railroad crossing problem is one of the most pressing in this country. No less than 230,000 grade crossings should be eliminated. At how many of these crossings have lives already been lost? How would the cost of these lives compare with that of eliminating the crossings? The total cost of the whole job would range from two to four billion dollars. It will have to be faced some time; why not in time to save thousands of human lives?

ARMORIES, CHURCH PEWS, HOSPITAL BEDS

Our deficiencies are greater now in private than in public buildings. We have continued, in spite of the emergency, to erect court-houses, post offices, jails, office buildings, armories, and libraries, and yet there are still not enough. But the shortage of schools and hospitals is more serious still. Of those already built many are badly in need of maintenance and sanitary improvements.

The emergency only emphasized the fact that the one-room school is an accompaniment of the unimproved road. Where good roads exist, we find more consolidated district schools with higher teaching standards and better sanitary facilities. But because local communities are not building new schools as fast as the old ones run down, the nation would have to build at several times the present rate to overtake our deficiency of four to five billion dollars in school construction.

The deficiency in hospitals and hospital equipment may approximate two billion dollars, according to studies made by the Milbank Memorial Fund, the Committee on the Cost of Medical

Care, and by other groups. There are today only one million beds in all the hospitals in the country and at least 400,000 more are needed. As a matter of fact, most cities are better supplied with church pews than with hospital beds, and some states would rather build armories. The over-all cost of necessary hospital expenditures would average $3,000 to $5,000 per bed.

The low income groups can rarely afford to live in new houses, but they pay dearly in health cost for having to live in unsanitary tenements, of which more than half are over thirty years old. The urban population alone needs more than eight million house units to replace sub-standard dwellings, while the rural population requires more than three million. In addition to replacements, of course, half a million new units would have to be built each year to care for the increasing number of families. The deficiency in urban and rural housing would therefore require public and private expenditures of billions of dollars.

These are estimates based on present methods of construction, but it is becoming ever more apparent that dwellings will have to be built more quickly and cheaply if housing is to remain a private enterprise. Today we are not even trying to keep pace with the loss of houses through obsolescence, fire, and decay. What is needed at once is a three-to-five billion dollar annual expenditure of public or private funds which would continue for the next decade. There is too much talk on the subject and too little construction of houses for the low income groups that are most in need of them.

Under the low rent housing program of PWA, fifty-one demonstration projects have been undertaken in thirty-six cities. These will provide shelter for 21,000 families. The Resettlement Administration (now the Farm Security Administration) has sponsored several suburban housing developments, including the much publicized Greenbelt, near Washington.

All the projects of PWA and RA together, though, do not constitute anything like an adequate approach to a problem which must be reckoned in terms of millions of dwelling units. It is expected now, with the passage of the Wagner Housing Act, that we shall see more federal housing. We should see more experimentation, too, since under this Act a dwelling unit may not exceed $1,000 per room or $4,000 for the unit. That provision may force the use of new materials and new methods.

FLOODS AND SEWERS

Periodically during the past four years the federal government has been called upon to relieve the suffering of people in drought or flood areas. In both cases the source of the trouble has been water; in one a lack of it, in the other, an overabundance. Too frequently these conditions are man-made, the consequence of too much farming in areas intended for grazing, of too much grazing in regions of sparse vegetation, and of a reckless denuding of the timber lands. Had the public domain, including the mountains, not been overgrazed and overcleared of timber by private interests, the ravages of the recent droughts would certainly not have been so severe. It will take years of labor to undo the damage man has wrought and prevent greater waste of our land resources.

That is why the government is now undertaking such an extensive program for flood and erosion control. Flood control, called "down-stream" engineering, is effected either by opening the channels so that surplus water can be carried away, or by developing flood reservoirs to regulate the flow. That was what was needed in the Ohio River Valley when the flood waters inundated large areas.

Erosion control is quite the reverse. It applies mainly to areas of low rainfall where the problem is to retain the water. One way to accomplish that is to encourage vegetation to grow and to restore the forests so that the rain may be absorbed where it falls. Then as much of the water as cannot soak into the ground in these dry areas should be stored in small reservoirs, where it may be used for irrigation. This procedure is called "up-stream" engineering.

In the fight against floods and soil erosion the government has enlisted the services of several federal departments. The Army Engineering Corps has estimated the work that will be needed to control flood waters on all the main river systems. The Soil Erosion and the Forestry Services have planned programs for the control of soil erosion.

As a means of utilizing unemployed labor, flood and erosion control projects offer administrative difficulties because of their isolation from the centers of population where relief workers are concentrated. The work, to be effectively carried on, must be done from camp locations such as the CCC boys work from now. This may eventually require a segregation of workers, reserving the camp projects for the young men and other non-family workers.

In urban centers the problem of water supply and sewage disposal presents many opportunities for public work. To bring in pure water and to remove sewage are expensive obligations which are no longer being adequately met by many cities. In the interest of community health, funds must be made available to them. This, in turn, suggests other related fields for public spending — malaria control, mosquito control, garbage disposal, and projects for screening homes against flies. One definite health-insurance project is the building of privies; over a million of them have been constructed under federal direction and distributed to private homes.

Who can say how much money needs to be spent for sewerage, drainage, and general sanitation? Every river system is a problem in itself, although the greatest health hazards are the rivers into which some cities dump their sewage at points above those where other cities draw drinking water. Eventually the rivers and beaches will have to be cleaned up. Would it not be worth the cost to have the waters of the Hudson River and the coast line from Coney Island to the Atlantic rendered free of pollution?

Water mains and sewers are parts of a single system of supply and disposal. Because both are so closely associated with the streams and rivers, and so obviously related to general health, their maintenance becomes a national as well as local problem. The time has come for the federal government to take a greater part in assuring cities an adequate water supply and thus to check the rising struggle for the river basins. The sewage problem is likewise one of national importance. Actually, millions of man-years of labor will be needed to make living in cities safe.

THAT AMERICA MAY PLAY

The public highways and the various systems of trails in mountains and forests are themselves recreational facilities. But when the traveler sets out to swim, play games, hunt, fish, or perhaps only to eat his lunch in the shade, another type of facility is needed: parks and playgrounds. Cities have recently become very active in providing such recreation space out of town. Bear Mountain Park and Jones Beach, for example, are New York City's playgrounds, although both are far removed from the city limits. On a more extensive scale, the national parks in the western states serve the same purpose.

We have no current data on which to base our estimates of the country's public recreational needs. We do know, however, that in no city is there adequate park or playground space. At the present time, in 898 municipalities, there are about 300,000 acres of parks and playgrounds, representing a public investment of $3,000 or more per acre. Yet if the park and play area were doubled, it would still not be too extensive for the needs of certain crowded communities.

The Report of the National Survey of Potential Product Capacity, sponsored by the New York City Housing Authority and the Emergency Relief Bureau of New York City in 1935, shows that recreational expenditures in the United States for 1929 were in excess of six billion dollars, of which about two billion went to the movies. The Survey estimated that in 1935 at least 85,000,000 people were underserved recreationally and that if the poor had had the same facilities as the middle class the expenditures in 1929 would have been twelve billion dollars.

To meet the deficiencies in public recreation would call for expenditures in excess of two billion dollars annually, and would provide annually more than a million man-years of labor.

As with any other type of construction project, the major part of the expense for recreational facilities begins only after the building is done. Once the parks, playgrounds, swimming pools, stadia, and other facilities are there, the community must face the expense of maintaining and operating them. It is because many local communities have been too slow in assuming this burden, that such an extensive recreational program has had to be carried on under WPA.

QUACKS, MIDWIVES, AND WITCH-DOCTORS

Great as is the lack of hospitals in the United States, the deficiency in hospital services, in clinics, and in general medical care, is even greater. According to the National Survey of Potential Product Capacity, families with incomes of less than $1,200 per year "are able to pay for only *one-sixth* of the nursing, *one-fourth* of the eye care, *one-third* of the dental care, and *two-thirds* of the surgical and hospital care that families in the higher income brackets can afford." Lacking the money to buy scientific care, the poor are forced to resort to quacks, patent medicines, midwives, and witch-doctors.

Paradoxically, while all these people lack proper medical care, at least half the doctors, dentists, and nurses in the United States do not have enough paying patients to provide them with a fair living.

Of the health provisions and health requirements for the country, the National Survey of Potential Product Capacity has made certain estimates on the basis of 1929 figures. These estimates, which follow, were compiled by the Survey from the report of the Committee on the Cost of Medical Care and from other reliable studies:

	Number 1929	Number Required
Physicians (practicing)....................	142,000	171,848
Dentists	62,400	121,081
Nurses (graduate and public health).........	293,800	270,150
Nurses (practical)........................	150,000	250,000
Pharmacists	132,000	150,000
Midwives	47,000	30,000

The cost of all medical care in 1929, based on various estimates, was $3,316,000,000, or about $26 per capita. The estimated requirements for 1935 were $5,136,000,000, or $42 per capita. The deficiency of $16 per person must be made up.

If millions of people could not pay for medical care in 1929, we may assume that millions more cannot pay for it today. We know now that such a situation, if permitted to continue, not only inflicts losses upon every community in which these people live, but brings about a dangerous lowering of the entire nation's health standards.

In January, 1938, reports of a survey made by the National Institute of Health of the United States Public Health Service revealed that in the population on relief was found the highest frequency rate in the country for both acute and chronic illnesses during 1935. Illnesses disabling for one week or longer occurred among relief families at a rate fifty-seven per cent higher than among families with incomes of $3,000 or over. In families just above the relief level, but under $1,000 a year, the illness rate was less than in relief families, but it was seventeen per cent higher than in the $3,000 class. In the latter group chronic disability kept only one family head in 250 from seeking work, whereas the same cause rendered one out of every twenty heads of relief families unemployable.

And not only do relief and low-income families experience more frequent illness during a year than their more fortunate neighbors, but their illnesses are, on the average, of longer duration, often running as high as sixty-three per cent longer.

In a surveyed population of 280,073 persons in eight large cities where such data was available, the average case of disabling illness in families with incomes of $3,000 and over received 5.7 calls from a physician, compared with 3.9 calls per case in relief families. The upper-income families thus received forty-six per cent more medical service per illness. In this connection the report pointed out that in 1935, the approximate year of the survey, a relatively large amount of medical care was being financed from relief funds, but that federal subsidies for medical care have since been discontinued.

A study of the country's death rate released in October, 1937, revealed an even more alarming situation. The death rate among the forty to fifty million Americans with incomes of $1,000 or less from the diseases that cause three out of every four deaths in the United States was twice that of the balance of the population. The death rate from tuberculosis alone was seven times as great among unskilled as among professional workers. Tuberculosis is the price the poor pay for inadequate food, inadequate shelter — and unceasing worry.

It is time we recognized the fact that if masses of the people cannot pay for health examinations and health care, these services will have to be provided for them. To meet our health obligations adequately would involve an outlay in public funds of not less than a billion dollars a year, which would be a good investment in national defense as well as national health.

In the field of education, estimates on our annual deficiency, quite apart from school buildings, range from three to eleven billion dollars. The estimates, of course, vary as they include or exclude various functions of education, or as they differ in the standards they set for salaries.

In 1929 student enrollment in all educational institutions was 29,900,000; in 1934 it was 30,500,000. Instructors in all institutions numbered 1,037,000 in 1929, and 1,042,000 in 1934. Most of these were in elementary and secondary schools.

According to reports of the United States Office of Education, there is a shortage of at least 200,000 teachers in our public schools. One teacher out of every three in the United States is working for less than $750 a year, and 90,000 rural teachers in 1933 were receiving less than $450 a year. From 300,000 to 1,000,000 children were actually denied their right to an education when many of our schools closed their doors during the depression. Between 1930 and 1933, owing to shortage of funds, the cost per child per school day had been reduced from sixty-three to forty-nine cents. And although expenditures for education in 1934 were $3,380,-000,000, educators all agree that they should have been much greater.

To meet these deficiencies in part at least, and to keep schools open in many places, the federal emergency program has allocated funds for supplementary teaching. FERA and, more recently, WPA have given financial support to nursery schools, to projects for adult education, workers' education and other types of instruction, in order that the services of thousands of jobless teachers may be utilized.

"ONE-THIRD OF THE NATION"

In 1934, the Brookings Institution published *America's Capacity to Consume,* summarizing the salient facts about income and expenditure for different classes of people. Some of these figures are pertinent to our discussion.

When the families and individuals in the United States are classified in broad income groups, it appears that:

  35.7% of the population live in minimum comfort on incomes from $1,500 to $3,000, and
  40.6% of the population live at subsistence and poverty levels on incomes under $1,500.

The lower group, which concerns us most, is composed of more than 11,000,000 families and individuals without families, as follows:

5,779,000 families and non-family individuals with incomes of less
than $1,000 per year, and
5,754,000 families and non-family individuals with incomes from
$1,000 to $1,500 per year.

The average income of nearly six million families and individuals without families was about $650 per year, or $300 less
than the Brookings Institution estimated as a "liberal diet" for a
family of five. Based on 1929 prices, the study placed the "liberal"
family diet at $950 for a year and supplemented that with a leaner
estimate of $800 for an "adequate diet."

If such estimates mean anything at all, they clearly indicate that
at least five million families are living at a level considerably below
a decent standard. In line with this conclusion the Brookings Institution pointed out that if all the below-subsistence families were
to enjoy a "liberal diet" there would need to be "an increase in the
production of all kinds of consumers' goods and services by something like seventy or eighty per cent."

At this point we come up against the dilemma which confronts
the federal work relief program. Most of the families supported by
federal work relief, and no less than three million other families
comprising more than twenty million persons, are living below a
decent level. If all these sub-marginal families could enjoy the
"liberal diet," there would be no surplus of food. If they could all
be decently clothed, there would be no surplus of raw materials,
and especially none of cotton.

But what is to be done when we are not permitted to use relief
labor for the production of the very goods which the sub-marginal
families need?

Let us see what happened to a social experiment intended to
relieve the market of surplus cotton in 1934. The government purchased 2,000,000 bales of cotton, and no one raised the slightest
objection. The government's next step was to find uses for the
surplus cotton that would keep it from entering into competition
with other finished products.

The most obvious solution was to convert the cotton into mattresses and quilts, making them with relief labor and distributing them to the needy. Immediately a chorus of protests went up from the mattress manufacturers and from other industrialists who were afraid of what federal mattress-making might lead to. The officials of FERA reassured them that the mattresses would be given to families that did not have mattresses and would certainly not be able to buy them.

The government discovered that mattresses could be made with unskilled labor. Mattress-making required very simple equipment and was, moreover, good work for unemployed women. More than two million mattresses were manufactured by the unemployed, and distributed to the poor. The mattresses were well made; so well made, in fact, that the manufacturers complained they were too good and would not wear out as quickly as commercial mattresses. It was bad for business. And so the project was discontinued. There was, unfortunately, no pressure brought by organized labor or anyone else to keep it going.

But the government did not stop using the surplus cotton to make quilts and comforters. That work is still going on, with the result that several million quilts have already been made and distributed to relief families.

THE PRODUCTS OF THEIR LABOR

How can the problem of enforced shortage be met, and how long can it be avoided? We can build roads or public buildings with relief labor, but not houses for the poor. We can use relief funds for education, but very little for medical care. We can build swimming pools to keep the children cool in summer, but every obstacle is put in the way of our making clothes to keep them warm in winter.

On a small scale the unemployed on projects are permitted to make clothing and bedding, and some are even allowed to preserve or bottle fruits and vegetables, but at best these efforts fall tragically short of meeting existing needs. The workers on relief are still unable to buy the products of their labor.

Underlying this situation, of course, is the fact that private industry has a proprietary stake in houses, clothing, food, and even in medical care. Proprietary interests would thus be injured if the government tried to supply deficiencies in these fields. It would, we are told, be contrary to American tradition.

In the meantime the people, millions of them, do not have enough food, clothing, or livable houses. Private industry, at the same time, has the capacity to produce large quantities of goods but it does not do so because not enough people have the money to buy what they need.

At least five million families at the bottom of the economic scale could use each year from $300 to $500 more goods per family than they now use. This would mean less than two dollars per day in increased consumption for families now earning less than $650 per year. But for the national income it would mean an increase of billions of dollars expended for goods and services. There can not be any real prosperity until this problem of distribution has been met in positive fashion.

It is easy enough to imagine the work a man can do in a year, but far more difficult to visualize how great is the loss to the nation as a whole of 50,000,000 irrecoverable man-years of labor not used over a period of six years. If some of that lost labor had gone into medical care, how much healthier would all the people be? How much lower would be the death rate of infants and mothers, or the incidence of sickness? Had some of the lost labor gone into manufacturing and building, how much better would the people be clothed and housed?

A conservative estimate for making up all deficiencies that might have been, and still may be, publicly met would approach ten billion dollars per year. That, however, may well be more than the federal and local governments will ever be willing to spend. And meanwhile the relief-recovery program must worry along, expending far less than is needed while so much work still waits to be done.

V. THE "USEFUL AND NON-COMPETITIVE" BOGEY

THE SOCIAL TEST

How far should the government go in giving jobs to the jobless?

Consider the carpenter who wrote to WPA: "I was working on WPA, but they laid me off and told me to go to a PWA job. When I went there the contractor on PWA wouldn't hire me because I was over fifty years old, and now can I get my WPA job back?"

What answer can be given to the carpenter? He is a willing and capable worker and he will be for perhaps fifteen years or more. If boom times were to bring about a labor shortage the contractor might hire him. But these are not boom times. Occasional odd jobs are the best the carpenter has been able to get. Public work of the relief type is preferable and more secure.

At the other end of the age scale is the young man who complained, as many young men can: "I tried to get a job everywhere but I can't find anything. They won't take me on WPA because I can't get certified for relief. At the Welfare Bureau they won't put me on relief because they say I don't have any dependents and I ought to be able to find something to do."

What answer can be given to a young man wasting his best years in idleness and getting neither work experience nor training? To tell him to find a job when there is none is an evasion. When there is work to be had in private industry he may be expected to take it. If it cannot be found, even by a diligent searcher, the young man's

CCC boys in Ohio go to school. Such instruction may help them to find jobs later on. Nearly two million men and women have enrolled in WPA adult education classes. In three years 700,000 adults have learned to read and write.

Geography for the blind. For the benefit of 125,-
000 blind persons in the United States, WPA has
maintained projects for writing books and making
maps in Braille. Much of this work was done by
unemployed blind workers. Ten thousand specially
constructed gramophones for reading to the blind
have been made for the Library of Congress to
lend to blind persons.

CCC boys near Washington, D. C., learn about tractors. During four years, 1,600,000 boys and young men have enjoyed the work and experience benefits of CCC. They have learned about work, but too few of them have learned skills that have labor market value.

Under the guidance of WPA artists, members of
the Paragon Boys Club, New York City, get lessons
in mural painting.

NYA girls learn dressmaking. For girls of this age group the federal work program has offered nothing comparable to CCC. Yet in every state are thousands of girls very much in need of work experience and training.

A low-price house in Alabama made of rammed earth. The Resettlement Administration has revived an ancient method of building houses. The gravel and clay walls are cool in summer and warm in winter. The cost of material and labor is low. The houseless poor could use a million houses of rammed earth or other inexpensive materials, but there would be opposition from the building industry.

PWA low-rent housing at Miami, Florida. These
small houses rent for about $5.50 per room per
month, which, cheap as it is, is not cheap enough
for the low income families in Florida.

The Cedar Central Apartments erected in Cleveland by PWA at a cost of $3,384,000. It replaces eighteen acres of slums—an eloquent illustration of work yet to be done. If this project were multiplied a hundredfold there would still be millions living in substandard houses. On their present incomes the slum dwellers could not afford to live in model houses.

Bluebeard Castle on the Virgin Islands. With WPA
funds this old landmark has been remodeled into
a hotel.

PWA has built or is building 204 bridges which will cost about $685,000 each. WPA has built 19,200 bridges which will cost from $3,000 to $15,-000 each, and has constructed 183,000 culverts along public highways.

The city hall at Pawtucket, Rhode Island, on the bank of the Seekonk River. This was a PWA job, one of 314 city halls and courthouses erected by PWA.

WPA built this city hall at Casa Grande, Arizona. Big cities can afford to borrow PWA funds for public buildings. Little cities need public buildings, too, but they are often too poor to borrow. In two years WPA has constructed 11,100 small public buildings.

PWA piers in New York City—big enough for the biggest ships. The five in dock are from top and left: Europa, Rex, Normandie, Georgic, and Berengaria.

Tragedy in the wake of a storm. WPA workers uncovering the wreckage of a truck in which the driver was killed. For emergency work in fires, floods, and hurricanes, or for cleaning up afterward, WPA and CCC have functioned as a work army.

After the flood in a Kentucky town. WPA workers
cleaning up the wreckage in a residential district.
Here is a WPA service that nobody objects to.
Even those who at other times call relief workers
lazy are glad to have their services in an emergency.

A South Dakota stream dried up by the drought. Millions of cattle were moved by the government to other regions for food and water.

idleness widens from a matter of private to one of public concern.

Meeting the work needs of the unemployed is the social test of public work relief, but it raises the old question of private rights in the labor market. How can the government employ the jobless on useful and non-competitive projects — in accordance with its pledge to industry — without invading the realm of private enterprise? It is demanded of work relief that it be socially useful and yet not compete with private enterprise. The "socially useful" phase of that policy is a recognition of federal responsibility to the jobless worker and to the community. The "non-competitive" phase seems to recognize the proprietary right of private industry to exploit the labor market.

Can work be useful and yet non-competitive? Are not the two terms mutually contradictory? Is it not true that private employers could do most of the useful work undertaken by the government? The postal service is in competition with the express companies. The water systems in some large cities were once privately owned, and so were the public roads. The public bridge across the bay between San Francisco and Oakland is in direct competition with the private ferries.

Ever since their foundation, the national and state governments have been gradually forced to take over public functions, encroaching upon fields of private endeavor. Examples of such encroachment are found in public education, public health, and in such federal activities as the Government Printing Office. The useful work of the Forest Service, on the other hand, is accepted as non-competitive. Private industry does not regard as competitive, either, the maintenance and inspection of lighthouses, harbors, and inland waterways. But all of these — the postal service, education, public health, and the rest — are, significantly, non-profit or low-profit areas of activity.

When the Civilian Conservation Corps builds a highway or trail through the forest it is called public work. But building roads is also an important private enterprise. With unemployed labor WPA has erected public buildings including thousands of schools.

But the construction of buildings is traditionally the province of private enterprise.

It is not easy to distinguish competitive from non-competitive public work. Emergency public projects since 1933 have not followed the old public work practices. Many kinds of work once done by contractors are now being done by force account, the government acting as planner, work supervisor, and paymaster. For example, the sewer work in a large city was normally let by contract, but the city, six years behind in its sewer schedule, was unable to finance its construction as before. The work was therefore done as a work-relief force-account project. Since this was competitive activity it might seem to represent a loss to the contractors.

In building the sewers with relief labor, however, it was not the purpose of that city to enter into competition with the contractor. The work was done because jobs were needed for unemployed local workers. A contractor would not have been able to use the labor at hand. In order to make a profit he would have demanded the right to use his own workers. The city officials discovered, to their surprise, that by conserving materials and using a higher type of supervision they were able to lay the sewer by force account at a cost as low as the contract bid.

Thousands of small communities, in undertaking such small projects, have found that by using relief labor they achieve a double purpose. Not only do they get useful work done but they save on relief costs. That is the ultimate social test of work relief from the community viewpoint.

DANCING IN THE STREETS

The people of a southern town danced in the street most of the night. They had just finished paving Main Street, lifting it out of the mud and dust. The workers on the job contributed two days of labor without pay, working overtime to finish the pavement for the Saturday night party. While the Mayor spoke, at the start of the festivities, the relief workers who did the job occupied the seats of honor in front of the crowd. When the foreman's turn came to speak, he said, "The men were glad to have this work. It was done honestly. We saved money on everything possible. Now this town has a paved street that we have wanted for years. This is a gift from Uncle Sam."

It was not, of course, a gift, because the town put up twenty per cent of the cost; but hard times and the WPA did make the project possible. The town, far from being demoralized, began to display unheard-of civic pride. The owners of property along the paved street started painting their buildings and removing unsightly structures that had never before offended the eye. Property owners on side streets decided to agitate for sidewalks leading to the newly paved street. Within a year the town had more than fifty lawns that had not existed before. Now the townsfolk want the WPA to lay a sewer.

The officials of a small Oklahoma city wanted to use relief labor to build an armory, and in order to obtain community authorization for the purchase of materials, they called a public meeting. The leaders of the city's various clubs and organizations did not, it developed, see the need for an armory. The young people wanted a hall where they could hold dances, but spokesmen for the glee club and the town band preferred a hall with a stage where they could put on entertainments. The two women's clubs wanted a public building with a kitchen and a room for small meetings. The Mayor replied: "These things can all be added to the armory, but it looks as if we will have to call this building by another name."

After making four or five concessions to community groups with other plans, the National Guard finally suggested putting the rifle practice range in the basement. The building, however, was called an armory, and was so dedicated. After that new difficulties arose. The National Guard complained that the armory was in such demand for social functions that it was difficult to get the use of it for their purposes.

So, in that small city, the armory became a community building used by the Boy Scouts, the Girl Scouts, the Theatre Club and the Town Band, as well as by groups of women and young people for social gatherings. It could not have been constructed entirely by local contributions, and had it not been for available WPA labor it might not have been built for many years.

But there is another side to this project that deserves mention. The armory was built of stone, because stone could be brought in from the nearby hills. In the town were two stonemasons who had been jobless most of the time for more than ten years. They were put in charge of the stonework and several young men were assigned to help them. After the armory was finished the two stonemasons and their helpers were hired to do private stone jobs in the same community. Owners of two private residences, for example, put them to work building stone fences around their grounds.

A Colorado town employed relief labor on a new park project. Among the park's most popular recreational facilities were a swimming pool and a concrete dancing pavilion. Yet during the last political campaign an eastern newspaper ridiculed the project as a "boondoggle." The citizens so resented the story that they passed resolutions condemning the newspaper.

These are not isolated cases of the constructive services rendered by work relief projects. No resident of San Francisco or Oakland would question the service value of the bridge over the bay connecting the two cities, or of the monumental bridge over the Golden Gate, both of which were made possible by federal appropriations to relieve unemployment.

Small communities are just as proud as great cities to see their towns get new community buildings, pavements, sewers, or recreational facilities. Isolated farmers are the first to benefit whenever farm-to-market roads are built or surfaced, enabling them to get to town on stormy days.

THE CONSTRUCTION INDUSTRY IS NOT HAPPY

In pre-depression times private construction was a major industry in the United States. In 1928 the total volume of construction was more than eleven billion dollars, of which seventy-seven per cent was for private work. By 1936 the total dollar-amount of construction had come back to about seven billion dollars, of which only forty-four per cent was for private enterprise. Much of the fifty-six per cent of public construction in 1936 was being done, not by the construction industry, but by force-account methods with relief labor.

The following table shows the source of funds for construction in the United States for selected years:

Source of Funds	1929	1932	1936
Total: All Sources......	10,166,000,000	3,289,000,000	6,784,000,000
Federal	315,000,000	525,000,000	2,511,000,000
State and Local........	2,100,000,000	1,403,000,000	1,301,000,000
Private	7,751,000,000	1,361,000,000	2,972,000,000

It is easy to understand why building contractors, road builders, and other private interests that once made handsome profits out of the construction industry are unhappy when all the public construction is not done by contract. They had in 1936 about one-third the amount of private construction work that they had in 1929, and now they are getting less public work. Yet this same industry cannot or will not use relief labor.

The trend toward work relief is disturbing to private enterprise both for what it is and for what it may become. If public bodies learn to do work just as well by the force-account method as by contract, and if this type of work gets wide acceptance, it is likely to continue. Federal, state, and local public bodies are learning to plan and to supervise work, and they are learning how to do good work economically.

There might, it is true, be a more clearly defined division of labor between the two basic types of public work. Although the building and construction industry should not monopolize the benefits of an unemployment program, it is perhaps entitled to its share. Expensive construction projects do give employment to workers who need jobs and they do create a considerable amount of indirect employment. But they are still not adequate for the purposes of a government that must recognize the rights of millions of workers who need special consideration if their labor is to be effectively utilized.

In attempting to cater to so many conflicting views on the work issue, the federal unemployment program has attempted to make too little money go too far. For example, when the present Works Program began, large sums of money were allocated to the federal agencies doing big expensive projects. Then came the winter of 1935–1936. The contractors on public buildings, dams, and other big projects having a per man-year cost of $1,600 and over, closed down completely because they could not operate at a profit. The workers they laid off had to return to WPA, where it was necessary to give them employment on force-account projects. Just at the time when the workers taken originally from relief rolls needed work most, the contractors could not or would not use them and WPA had to. Then the critics of WPA said, "See how inefficient the work is?"

There is another aspect of the same difficulty. When WPA was trying to employ about eighty per cent of the unemployed, it was receiving only about forty per cent of the funds allocated for all the workers on the program. WPA has, in fact, been confronted with the task of providing employment for relief workers at a per man-year expenditure for the United States of less than $800 for labor, supervision, equipment, and materials. In some states the per-man limit per year has been as low as $400. Better work could certainly be done if a little more money were available for the utilization of relief labor.

BOONDOGGLING PROJECTS

The work relief division of the Works Program has had to find types of work that would utilize many occupations and skills not usually found on regular public work. It is these unusual projects, in fact, which often come nearest to meeting the government's pledge to industry to do only non-competitive work. If a project is useful it is sure to be criticized because it is competitive, while if it is non-competitive it is just as likely to be condemned by the same critics for not being useful.

The term "boondoggling" may have had other origins, but it derives its present connotation from an investigation into relief projects in New York City. Hostile elements there charged that too much money was being spent on useless projects in such fields as health, education, recreation, and research. It does not matter, now, that the findings of the investigation were favorable to the work; the term is still used to discredit certain types of relief jobs.

"Boondoggling" is one answer to a serious contemporary problem. Technological advances in factory and office are constantly disemploying large numbers of workers, and despite assurances from American business that new industries will spring up, creating new occupations and new jobs, the truth is that such few new industries as there are do not want the unemployed from the relief rolls. In fact, no matter how many new industrial processes are developed, many of the unemployed will still have to be retained on public work.

And what of non-industrial pursuits? Acting, for example. In a depression actors are naturally among the first to suffer. In 1929 the demand for their services fell off soon after the market crash. Many of the theatres that closed then have never reopened. It is, incidentally, a sorry commentary on our democracy that even in good times the legitimate theatre and the opera were out of reach of the vast majority in the United States, and that thousands of competent actors were even then without an audience.

The federal government set a memorable precedent when it undertook to employ actors at their own occupations. That, too, was called "boondoggling." But despite all criticism, the theatre projects have won wide approval.

Musicians, too, have shared in the new government program.

Under federal auspices highly trained orchestras, soloists, choral and chamber music groups have played to packed houses in thousands of concerts from coast to coast. For the first time music other than radio music was made available to the people at prices they could afford.

Creative artists, including sculptors, have always had a hard time making a living in the United States. Art has been raised to the luxury level, as something to be enjoyed by the rich alone. In the meantime, art schools have been graduating hundreds of artists every year, only to see them go hungry because no one will pay for their products. Yet while all this talent was going to waste, thousands of persons in this supposedly culturally advanced nation had never seen an original canvas or water color.

In the Federal Arts Project, the Government, recognizing the need of jobless artists, put them to work according to their special skills. Today their paintings — thousands of them — hang in public places where everyone may see them. Hundreds of their murals add beauty and color to the hitherto drab walls of public buildings. This is more "boondoggling."

IS CULTURE PUBLIC WORK?

Consider the architects. Theirs is a service, like the building of low-cost houses for the poor, that has been too long neglected. Of teachers, too, there is ever a supply far in excess of the demand. Yet in the face of a growing need for teachers, the teaching profession has waited in vain for jobs. The federal government has accepted part of the responsibility by putting teachers to work on such "boondoggling" projects as teaching the blind and the mute, training handicapped and backward children, giving vocational guidance, providing adult education in music and arts, and offering courses for underprivileged workers and the unemployed.

Slowly and almost grudgingly public recreation is being recognized as a necessity. Millions of people living in congested urban quarters have very definite recreational needs which have been met only partly. Under the work relief program unemployed recreational instructors have been put on the job in playgrounds, athletic fields, swimming pools, and gymnasia, supervising youngsters at play and thus keeping them off the streets. In many cities, playgrounds, pools, and other facilities would never have been built were it not for the federal projects. This is what some people call "boondoggling"; but the government would provoke more criticism today if it attempted to curtail this program than was ever expressed in the course of establishing it.

The private labor market has not yet absorbed still other groups of professional, technical, and white-collar workers. Thousands of expensively trained doctors, lawyers, nurses, and dentists have been condemned to idleness. But when the government sponsored health projects that would enlist the services of nurses, doctors, and dentists, some who professed to fear the coming of socialized medicine opposed the projects as competitive.

Thousands of unemployed white-collar workers have been engaged in cataloguing the records of local, state, and federal bureaus and departments. Valuable historical information has been recovered and filed, or made available to libraries and museums. Hundreds of writers have been put to work compiling that most important of publishing ventures, *The American Guide,* while more than a hundred local guidebooks will eventually be issued for the states and for some of the leading cities.

But all of these are cultural projects which some critics would never approve as public work. They honestly believe public money should not be spent on the arts or on research, no matter how valuable the results to communities or to the nation as a whole.

However, the "boondoggling" projects are not all in the cultural fields. In New York City a research project to discover water-leaks more than paid for itself. Many cities and counties have sponsored tax surveys which have often brought to light enough untaxed or undertaxed property to more than justify the project's cost. Geological surveys have uncovered a number of hitherto unsuspected natural resources. Other profitable studies have been made in plant disease, soil conservation, and in the production of materials which normally have to be imported.

In no field of public enterprise, however, have the processes of public education been more extensive and vitalizing than in that of unemployment relief. Thousands of communities have learned under federal supervision to do things that were never done by government in this country before. There is every indication that the people themselves are vitally interested in doing more, and that their confidence in democratic government is growing.

LABOR – A PERISHABLE COMMODITY

In this public educational process the federal government has never been more responsible or responsive to the wishes of the people than in the program for the unemployed. No phase of the New Deal program for recovery has invaded the old order of things more than has work relief, yet no phase of this program has moved with more caution and respect for the old order.

It is true that the government pledged itself not to compete with private enterprise in its work program for the unemployed. It is also true that this pledge has not been fully kept, and cannot be. To keep such a pledge would not only be of doubtful benefit to industry, but if literally kept it would be a serious invasion of the inherent rights of those workers who cannot get private employment.

When the livestock was dying in the drought region, the federal government launched a buying program in which it purchased millions of head of cattle and sheep. Some were killed on the spot for their hides; some were transported to good pasture land; others were slaughtered for meat which was packed in cans for distribution to the unemployed. The cattle program was an emergency measure for saving a resource and preventing a loss. There was, nevertheless, a certain amount of unavoidable loss which was shared by all the people. But had the government's purchase plan not been put into effect, the loss, and the suffering, too, would have been far greater for having been concentrated in one area.

Federal work relief for the unemployed is another kind of buying program. It permits the labor of idle workers to be purchased and put to use rather than wasted. If private industry will not or cannot buy the labor of the jobless and the government does not, it must waste away, since labor is a perishable commodity. But the labor of the unemployed cannot be wasted without leaving a fearful cost behind. In the long run the cost of the idleness of these workers is visited on society as a whole in lowered living standards and in the loss of the many valuable services they might have contributed.

As between the responsibility of the government for using the labor of the unemployed and the pledge to industry not to use it in competition, the choice is probably largely one of policy. Not to use this labor would be an arrant waste of human material, in view of the many types of public work and the great volume of it that is waiting to be done.

It would be false economy to deny the unemployed the right to work and it is equally false economy to leave undone the work already too long delayed.

VI. PAYING THE BILL

"SOMETHING OUGHT TO BE DONE ABOUT IT"

People like our economics professor, who worry about the national debt, are more anxious than ever today, because for more than three years the expenditures of the federal government have exceeded revenues by more than three billion dollars each year. There is, furthermore, no prospect of the expenditures and receipts being balanced very soon.

Here are the figures for three years ending 1936:

General expenditures.............	$11,075,000,000
Emergency expenditures...........	10,949,000,000
Total Government expenditures (1934, 1935, 1936)..........................	$22,024,000,000
Receipts of the Government (1934, 1935, 1936)..........................	11,032,000,000
Deficit for 1934, 1935, 1936.......................	$10,992,000,000

The deficit for three years thus about equals the amount spent for emergency relief and recovery purposes, a coincidence which seems to support the conclusion that the budget could be balanced if emergency expenditures were eliminated. But the whole story is not told in these figures. Many general functions of the government have been carried on with emergency funds, and many states and cities have drawn liberally on them to meet their obligations.

The debate about government economy is carried on between those who would balance the budget by reducing expenditures and those who dare to think of increasing taxes. Significantly enough, the champions of reduction are also the leaders in the fight against any increase in relief expenditures.

When the bill to appropriate $1,500,000,000 for work relief was before Congress, opposition was loud and bitter at first. Then President Roosevelt asked Congress for legislation to deal with wealthy tax dodgers. At once there was stunned silence in the ranks of the rich, whose hundreds of incorporated yachts and personal holding companies have been convenient devices for evading taxes.

The problem of balancing the budget is not serious in a land where so much wealth accumulates and, through legal legerdemain, escapes taxation in the process. If this government taxed wealth as some governments do, the budget could be balanced in one year and the debt could be wiped out in a very few more. Much of that huge debt is owed by the government to the very men of wealth who were suddenly silenced by the President's plea for laws to handle tax dodgers.

There is little point, however, in demanding a just tax system unless the government stands ready to impose upon itself every possible economy, both by avoiding unwarranted spending and by curtailing the giving of benefits wherever it can. Nevertheless, in spite of all economies, government expenditures must inevitably become greater each year. As more people demand more services, federal and local agencies have to be expanded to provide these services.

When the government was piling up its greatest previous debt, during the World War, there was no outcry then for "economy." That, of course, was different. The difference, however, lay chiefly in the economic status of the recipients of government benefits.

Those into whose pockets war profits flowed most plentifully are the ones who, today, are deploring "government spending."

WITHOUT HUMILIATION

Whether a government bestows tariff benefits on the rich or relief benefits on the poor, it may do too much or too little. If one set or class of people is given too much, an injury is imposed upon others. Business groups in this country, for example, have generally won their demands, whether for higher tariffs or, as in the airplane, automobile, and shipping industries, for billions in indirect subsidies. Can the government now deny the unemployed the financial assistance that will guarantee their right to work?

Emergency relief and public work were put into effect primarily as national substitutes for the old local welfare, but they differ from it in being more businesslike and constructive in character. Federal welfare has taken some of the sting out of applying for public assistance, and that is what so many prosperous people object to. They want to make certain that the person who gets relief shall suffer humiliation in the process.

In another sense, too, federal welfare activity is disturbing. Hidden away in three thousand counties and twenty thousand towns, the aggregate cost of caring for the needy was not known in former years and was not calculated on a national scale as it is now. Since the national government has begun to share the cost more people are aware of it and are made uneasy. They watch the rising national debt and begin to wonder how and by whom the bill will be paid.

It must be borne in mind, first, that the federal government did not take over responsibility for relief until all the other agencies had obviously failed. Ever since it assumed that burden, the government has consistently tried to withdraw its support and to pass the responsibility back to the states and localities. Yet every attempt it has made to abandon the emergency unemployment program has been fought both by the localities and by the unemployed. Hostile interests have thus been able to make it appear that the government has not been sufficiently hard-boiled and aggressive in ridding itself of the relief burden.

A private charitable agency in a large eastern city recently made an appeal for contributions, using this argument: "400,000 families are in need and too proud to submit to public relief." The very businessmen who support such a charity in this statement are trapped in a contradiction of their own making. They have said on many occasion that too much money is being spent on public relief. Then, as sponsors of charity, they publicly admit that in a single city 400,000 families are in need. The contradiction means only that the sponsors of that charity believe that haphazard private relief is better. Whether it is or not, we do know that private relief is sketchier, which may be the reason why many persons of wealth prefer it.

CHARITY AND THE DOLE COME DEAR

We should not forget what relief was like during those dark days prior to 1933. In every community, groups were organized to beg old clothes for the poor. Nobody in any city then was saying that 400,000 families were in need, but were "too proud to submit to public relief." Instead, they were begging from door to door, glad to obtain leavings. At least one high public official in Washington approved a plan for a systematic gathering of the refuse from clubs, hotels, and restaurants to be distributed through soup kitchens. He said nothing of public work. Only the unemployed were asking for that.

If people have to be helped because they cannot get work, we are faced with a condition and not with a theory. Whether there is a public dole or only private charity, whether there is work relief or none at all, people will quite properly demand the right to live. They do go on living, wearing ragged clothes, sleeping in slums, eating inferior food, and getting indifferent medical care. Even in 1931 and 1932 millions of unemployed were living, but how they lived is no credit to our vaunted American civilization.

Twenty per cent or more of the population was being carried along by all possible expedients, including mendicancy. Organized private charity was of little help because with so little money and so many to feed charity had to be spread too thin. Our faith in private charity cost us dear in those depression years. We know now that while the unemployed waited for charity the cost of their idleness was piling up, and that much of it was being passed back to society. These are some of the costs that have been paid or still wait to be paid:

1. The cost of organized private charity which for all its moral and disciplinary implications did not meet the need.
2. The cost to individuals who loaned money, made personal gifts, or gave board and rent to unemployed friends or relatives.
3. The cost of local public relief or work relief defrayed out of the tax funds of states and localities but later supplemented by federal funds also paid from taxes.
4. The negative costs reckoned in terms of the increase of crime, juvenile delinquency, vice, sickness, slum crowding, and other degrading accompaniments of social demoralization. Most of these costs have been unloaded on the children of the unemployed.
5. The costs of working in sweatshops and of taking jobs at less than a living wage. Such costs bring about a lower standard of living and are passed on to all producers.
6. The costs of not training the youth, resulting in lessened self-confidence and self-respect of workers who have learned no skills, a burden that all society must share.

While these and other costs of wholesale idleness accumulated, we still heard the strident voices of those who believed that the situation might have been met with a little more charity. Perhaps, but at what a price!

THE POOR TAKE CARE OF THE POOR

Private charity is sometimes called the rich man's gift to the poor. True, a few excessively rich individuals do give away large amounts out of their incomes, but on the whole, according to a recent survey, the total gifts of all who filed income tax returns have never amounted to as much as two per cent of their income, even in prosperous years. The wealthiest members of a community usually lend their names to any fund-raising drive, but that is frequently their only contribution. It is well known among people engaged in raising money for charitable purposes that, in proportion, the poorer classes are always the more generous.

The most important levy placed directly on the poor is the loss that all workers must bear when the unemployed among them cannot buy the products of their labor. Employers lose, too, from a contraction of the market, but the major share of the loss is passed down to the workers. Thus the burden of poverty lies heaviest on those nearest the brink of unemployment.

In any scheme for sharing the cost of poverty the poor are bound to carry the load. They are closer than the rich to the unemployed. The jobless workers are their relatives or friends, with intimate claims on them, and what they give to help the jobless they have no hope of getting back. Nor have they much hope of themselves escaping the abyss of poverty if their meager surplus goes regularly to help others in greater need.

If, on the other hand, the unemployed are given public relief or work, the situation is different. The funds to maintain a public work program are either obtained by taxation or are borrowed by the government. If the money comes out of immediate tax levies, there is greater prospect of the burden's being equitably distributed, provided only that measures other than property or sales taxes are resorted to. If the money is borrowed, it will have to be paid back out of future taxes.

Money borrowed for welfare purposes is money borrowed by the people from themselves. Generally it is the wealthy who buy government and municipal bonds, and it is the wealthy who get the usufructs from them in interest and tax exemption. Thus the money obtained from the sale of bonds is really borrowed from the rich.

The well-to-do say of the public debt: "Our children will have to pay this bill." That is true; the children of the rich — and of the poor, too — will have to pay the bill. We don't know yet how the burden will be distributed among them but we do know that when the public debt is liquidated the money will return to the rich or to their children.

LOCAL MEDICINE FOR NATIONAL ILLS

The cost of caring for the unemployed is a particularly live issue because there is no agreement on how or by whom it should be paid. Shall the burden be carried by citizens according to their wealth? In that case most of the money would be collected in the big financial centers. Shall the money be collected by sales taxes? Then the poor would be taxed out of all proportion to their ability to pay.

There seems to be a rising disposition to levy taxes on profits and on accumulations of wealth rather than on the bread of the poor. It is, indeed, this very tendency that is causing the wealthy so much concern about the rising public debt.

The confusion about the unpaid bill is further intensified by the persistent drive to make unemployment relief a local matter. In the 1936 campaign, former President Hoover and Republican Presidential Candidate Alfred M. Landon made capital of the idea of passing the relief program back to the local communities.

The proposal would be sound enough if the wealth of the country were evenly distributed. Actually, however, a few states and cities are richer than all the others combined. It is even said that in one New York county alone is owned half the wealth of the United States.

One of the consequences of inadequate local relief is an increasing migration of the people. Because local public or private agencies take care of families first, single persons have to shift for themselves. They leave home and go to the cities, only to find the local agencies unwilling to help them because they are transients. Destitute families move from cities to live with relatives in the country.

Willy-nilly they manage somehow, although the cost of their idleness and need reappears in some form, often in losses that are spread subtly and invisibly over the years.

Defenders of the proposal to localize relief ignore the fact that in the world of finance there is no decentralized local control. Investment and banking affairs are managed from the great financial centers. It is generally conceded, indeed, that a Wall Street acre is the center of money control. In business, too, there is no local control over the type of goods or services produced, over the volume of production, the number of workers hired, the wages paid, or the price asked for the product. Local control of business would not only be impractical, it would be grossly wasteful.

Yet those who would not expect business or finance to be confined to county, municipal, or state control see no inconsistency in their demand that relief be returned to the local communities. Here is a national malady, nationally contracted, but the leaders of industry and finance want to cure the ailment with local treatment! It is hardly a debatable issue.

It is not debatable partly because all the local medicines were tried without success between 1929 and 1932, but largely because in 1932 the country awoke to the fact that the very security of the nation was at stake and that national measures were needed.

Many who have managed to preserve their old standard of living unimpaired have concluded that all the others might recover theirs if they were thrown on their individual resources. From this spurious reasoning, cherished largely by those who have escaped disaster, stems an uncompromising determination to pass the relief burden back to the localities and to the unemployed.

GHOST TOWNS

Since 1932 the federal government has appropriated eighteen to twenty billion dollars for (1) loans to business and agriculture to stimulate employment and to restore credit, (2) purchases of surplus goods to relieve glutted markets, and (3) direct relief and work for the unemployed. Although the sums of money appropriated for these emergency purposes were great, they did not equal more than half the loss of national income in 1932. People like the professor, who in 1932 were wondering when the spending would start, are now wondering when it will stop.

They are the people who fear they may in some intangible future be called on to pay more taxes. Many of them are well aware that in the past they have not always carried their full share. Through their lobbies in state capitols and at Washington they have managed to get the taxes they favor, taxes that rest on consumption more than on profits and surplus.

It is part of the public strategy of those who have come unscathed through the depression to express anxiety over the moral effects of relief on the unemployed. Such solicitude was recently professed by a leader of a business community who said: ". . . we must beware of pampering, and of rendering potentially useful citizens useless, by allowing them to assume that it is the government's function not only to meet pressing temporary emergencies, but to look after all their needs."

There can be little question of whose welfare such speakers are concerned with — their own, threatened by higher taxes, or that of the unemployed, for whom starvation is the sole alternative to relief. It is interesting to observe that the more fearful people are of federal taxation, the more favorable they are to local relief responsibility.

Unfortunately, most local communities lack the facilities either to impose or to collect adequate taxes. Very often they simply do not have the resources to tax; or, if they have the resources, they are not always willing to assume tax burdens that they can possibly dodge.

On its work and relief program the government has spent more than ten billion dollars. To match this, the states and municipalities have appropriated in labor, materials, equipment, and money less than three billion dollars. Some of the richer states have been able to meet the federal government half way in supporting the unemployed; other states, mainly in agricultural regions, have contributed next to nothing.

Every state has its bankrupt towns, stranded towns, and ghost towns. Some of them may at last be on the way to recovery, but they are still deep in debt. They cannot borrow more money. They hesitate to tax themselves more. In every state there are towns too poor even to maintain adequate police and fire departments or school systems. An extreme case was Key West, Florida, where four years ago there was no money with which to pay the public employees, and no money for garbage collection or for repairs to the city's fire signal system. Exposed to the hazards of fire and disease, the city and its people had to be helped by federal funds. It would be absurd to argue in favor of local relief responsibility for cities so poor.

In New England there are scores of towns whose industries once had large payrolls. The factories have long since closed; the people have no employment prospects; the towns have no credit. The goods that used to be produced in the factories were sent away to market or were stored in warehouses, while the profits gleaned from marketing them went to the cities, into the pockets of absentee owners who today do not approve public work. They oppose any increase in the bill for unemployment relief on the ground that taxpayers have "rights." Those are heedless citizens who would put the rights of a taxpayer above the rights of human beings to earn a decent living.

For the poor in thousands of bankrupt or abandoned towns one thing is certain. If they do not get federal aid, they will not get any. Yet there will be no escaping the bill for their idleness. The unemployed, with poetic justice, will return it to the owning class in the form of underbuying.

EVERYBODY LOSES

The mayor and alderman of any town, the commissioners of any county, and the officials of most states resort, in their negotiations concerning the financing of unemployment relief, to every possible device to get the federal government to pay the bill. They have been unusually successful, and often honest, in pleading poverty. Yet while many communities are still very poor, others are ceasing to be. As might be expected, the wealthy community is usually able to exert the greatest political influence, although on the whole the politically favored communities are relatively few.

Nevertheless, whether they can pay the bill for relief or not, or even carry a share of it, local political units will vie with each other to get control of the spending. If the money is to be used on public work projects they strive for as much administrative control as possible. In this they are not opposed by the federal government, provided the local administration meets the established standards and minimum rules of work integrity.

But however much they would like to do for the unemployed, local and state officials have not been able to resist the highly effective demands of the wealthy elements in every community to keep relief standards low.

It was almost entirely pressure from the federal agencies that brought the standards up. Federal initiative, influenced in many cases by labor support, raised the average work relief wage on WPA in 1935 to $50 a month, or $15 above the average relief budget under FERA. That is why the groups that cannot openly oppose an average monthly wage of $50 want relief to be locally administered. Obviously, most communities could not maintain the standards established by the federal government, nor, even if they were able to, could they resist the pressure to pull these standards down.

When the unemployed buy consumer goods it is the manufacturing and merchandising interests that gain. What a shock it would be to business if we really did turn back to the rugged individualism and relief standards of 1931! The owning groups would save money on taxes, but how much more would they lose in reduced sales and lowered profits? So, along whatever avenue we approach the problem we arrive at the same conclusion: The idleness of part of the workers becomes the loss of all workers and eventually, whether by federal taxation, local taxation, or no taxes at all, the cost of idleness is borne by everyone.

If in an unemployment relief program there has to be a choice between federal or local financial responsibility, the former appears to have the advantage both from the social and economic viewpoint. At the outset local relief seems to offer a deceptively easy escape. Federal relief, on the other hand, seems at first glance to cost more, especially if it takes the form of work relief. But there is this big difference: with work there is less loss through weakened morale, less eventual cost due to the loss of skill through idleness, and less waste as a consequence of planless and overlapping measures. If narrow-visioned business leaders could only see the wisdom in the government's program they would be less concerned about who will pay the bill and more concerned about getting all the unemployed to work.

VII. HOW MUCH UNEMPLOYMENT IS ENOUGH?

"THEY WON'T LEAVE THEIR WPA JOBS"

Newspapers in New York City and on Long Island recently carried stories about farmers who had been forced to import Negro agricultural labor from the South because workers on relief and on WPA would not accept farm employment. Press reports also stated that WPA rates of $4 per day made it difficult for the farmers to employ non-relief labor at $2 per day.

Investigation of the complaint disclosed that seventeen Negroes had been brought from the South by one Long Island farmer; that a similar number of Negroes had been imported in previous years; and that the wages paid these Negroes were not $2 per day but "$9 per week for six twelve-hour days and a package of cigarettes for overtime." And from this the sum of $17 for bus fare from the South was deducted.

Investigation also disclosed that Negroes brought in during previous seasons did not earn enough to support themselves and their families even while working, and that at the end of the season most of the imported Negroes were obliged to appeal for relief. From November, 1936, until April, 1937, the county expended $36,842 on relief for these imported agricultural workers or on their transportation home.

One newspaper, upon learning that there was another side to this complaint about a shortage of agricultural workers, sent a reporter out to investigate. He applied for work at fifteen different farms, always making it a point not to ask any questions about hours of work or wages. Not one of the fifteen farmers needed any labor.

Complaints about a labor shortage are usually made by two types of employers: those who will not pay a living wage, and those who want many applicants for each job they can give. During a reported "shortage" of wood choppers in northern New York, lumber interests appealed to the government for permission to bring in Canadians because American lumberjacks would rather work on WPA. Inquiry revealed that a plentiful supply of American workers was available to those companies that paid standard wages.

Each year the best sugar companies in Colorado and surrounding states make the same complaints about a labor shortage, and each year investigation has proved that beet growers willing to pay the prevailing minimum rates are able to get labor. The effect of such complaints has been to encourage the importation of Mexican workers from New Mexico. As a rule the rates of pay are so low that at the close of the beet season the workers usually find themselves penniless.

In August, 1937, a Los Angeles paper typically reported a shortage of 5,000 workers in the California hop fields, and stressed the unwillingness of 90,000 workers on relief rolls to take jobs. Investigation disclosed:

1. That there was an ample supply of labor available for the hop harvest.
2. That earnings were so low that none but experienced workers with the aid of their families could make a living.
3. That for workers imported into the region there were no camping or other shelter facilities.
4. That there was no local anxiety about the labor supply, and that the complaint originated 500 miles away.

RELIEF — A WHIPPING BOY

Rarely does the cry for help go up from other than the temporary marginal users of labor. Often such seasonal workers as they need are obliged to move to the site of the work or to travel long distances. The hours are long, the pay low, the conditions often degrading.

In the cotton fields of Texas 10,000 workers are wanted for ten or twenty days. In the berry fields of North Carolina 3,000 workers are needed (to work forenoons only). In the hop fields of California 5,000 workers are wanted. Workers are needed in the truck gardens of New Jersey, in the cane fields of Louisiana, in the cherry orchards of Michigan or the apple orchards of Oregon. Men are wanted to fish salmon, to cut pulpwood, to pack shrimp, to sell from door to door, to load or unload cars. Women are wanted for housework, to work in factories or in the fields.

In all these activities and occupations of seasonal or marginal character there are annual complaints of a labor shortage. But during the last three or four years the usual outcry has been supplemented by charges that relief or work relief or both make it impossible to get workers.

While most of the criticisms come from employers of seasonal agricultural labor, some do come from manufacturers. From May to August, 1937, WPA investigated one hundred cases in which WPA was accused of keeping workers off the labor market. In not a single instance were the charges substantiated by the facts. There was no shortage of labor except at less than subsistence wages or in cases where complainants had a reputation for not paying their employees at all.

Often, too, employers that complain about the shortage of workers and demand reductions in the relief rolls really want a special type of labor. They may need skilled workers, and finding that the skilled workers on relief are not the kind they want, they protest anyway. All such complaints, however unjustified, help create a bias against the workers on public projects, serving to set the relief population aside as a caste. The unemployed become a class about which very little is known but about which much ill is spoken.

It will make no difference if a thousand complaints of labor shortage lodged against WPA are investigated and found to be groundless. Charges that WPA is robbing the labor market will still be made as the seasons roll around.

This is probably inevitable because the federal relief program has invaded the sacred confines of the so-called free labor market. Some of the accusations concerning relief and work relief are made by people who honestly believe they have been injured by WPA. But most of the charges are made with mixed motives, by people who are using relief and work relief as a whipping boy.

WHAT IS THE FREE LABOR MARKET?

The labor manager of a chain of sugar factories was asked to join with WPA and the United States Employment Service in drawing up a labor agreement that would prevent the bringing of too many seasonal workers into some of the beet growing areas.

In response to the suggestion the sugar official said: "We will be glad to cooperate. All we want is a supply of labor where and when we need it."

He could not have made any other statement or taken any other position. So long as his company is in competition with other sugar companies, each must get its labor as cheaply as possible. Each wants access to a large and competent labor supply. The sugar official was concerned with making sugar to make a profit and he was not, like the representatives of the federal and state agencies, concerned with the welfare of his workers.

Later in the year when work in the beet fields began, the sugar official complained that WPA was making it difficult to get labor. Although all possible projects had been closed down and all the beet workers laid off by WPA, still the sugar company insisted that the existence of other WPA projects was interfering with the free labor market. The workers on WPA had, it is true, organized into a union of the unemployed that served to implant in the minds of the beet workers the idea of organization; and this, of course, was particularly disturbing to the sugar companies' concept of a free labor market.

The sugar official was asked what the policy of the government should be if in the autumn thousands of beet workers were left stranded without shelter, without clothing for their children, and without money for food. "What if 500 Mexican families brought in from New Mexico are stranded in Montana and Wyoming?" He replied: "To that I have no answer. My job is to get a supply of labor when and where it is needed."

The answer of the sugar official is the answer of all private enterprise: it simply cannot be responsible. Industry's demand for an ample supply of workers is in effect a demand that a large percentage of workers must be insecure and idle, but capable and willing to work. Industry is willing to let demand and supply regulate wages and working conditions, but always with the understanding that at any given time there shall be workers of the proper kind in greater numbers than are needed.

Such a free labor market is free only to those who can take advantage of it. To the vast army of the unemployed it resembles more a slave market. If every employer in every industry and if every farmer and trader could have the labor surplus demanded by the sugar official, the volume of unemployment would have to be great indeed.

For the sugar industry alone it would mean that a population numbering thousands of families must subsist on a sub-marginal level throughout the year in order to earn a few cents per hour in the fields during the beet season. Are the handsome profits of the beet sugar industry worth the sacrificing of so many human beings?

The same question could be posed with respect to hundreds of other industries that utilize cheap labor in abundance and prosper in direct proportion to the number of applicants for jobs. The government with its work program has frankly entered the field in an effort to shorten the hiring line and to relieve the misery of some of the unemployed and sub-marginal workers.

THE FREE LABOR MARKET?

The labor surplus is often called the pool of reserve labor. In the free, unregulated labor market any worker, according to his energy and ability, should be able to find work. The most efficient will get plenty, and others, depending on their efficiency or adaptability, will get less. Some will get high wages and others low wages, but for competitive labor to function as industry, in general, would have it there must be a complete absence of either union organization or unemployment relief.

Such a free market could exist only if a similar degree of competition existed between employers. As it is, monopolies, price fixing, production control, and trade agreements among industries that only pretend to be competitors have reduced the freedom of the labor market to a fiction. The labor pool at times has become a turbulent flood from which workers have been lucky to emerge with any livelihood at all.

Advocates of a free labor market could not tolerate one that distributed benefits equally, because that would give the workers more than the traditional amount of liberty and less than the traditional amount of insecurity.

When experts talk about the optimum labor market, they mean one that is neither overstocked nor undersupplied with good workers who have not been obliged to endure too much unemployment. In such a market the number of workers in the reserve pool should be sufficient to keep the economic forces in healthy balance. But that is precisely the kind of market the sugar official does not want for the kind of labor he needs.

We have not had an optimum market since 1929, and all industries, sugar included, have suffered in consequence. Millions of workers, first reduced to the level of begging for work, were eventually reduced to begging for food.

When, to relieve this situation, the government finally took a hand in providing relief and jobs, private industry was not at first opposed. But once the crisis had been averted by giving the jobless public work, the government was blamed for "interfering" with the labor market.

CATCH-AS-CATCH-CAN

Here are some figures from the United States Employment Service that show the extent of government "interference." During two years, ending June 30, 1936, the USES received 10,400,000 applications and was able to supply 8,900,000 jobs, of which 6,700,000 were jobs on relief or public work.

	Applications	*Placements*
Professional, technical, clerical workers, and salespersons	1,700,000	600,000
Skilled workers	1,600,000	840,000
Production workers, mostly factory labor	2,270,000	1,200,000
Personal service and domestic workers	1,900,000	1,100,000
Unskilled workers of all classes	1,950,000	4,645,000
All others	980,000	515,000

It is apparent from the above table that jobs in the skilled and technical fields are hard to get. The scarcity of demand, however, is more marked in industrial than in construction skills. Many professional and skilled workers were assigned to public employment; others had to be assigned to jobs as common laborers. Of these there were 4,645,000 placements — more than all other placements combined — and most of them on relief jobs.

There is the answer to employers who say there is a shortage of trained workers. Either they do not know of the employment service or they fail to make use of it.

The so-called labor pool comprises the total number of unemployed workers from which all employers secure the labor they need. The difficulty here is that no employer can say exactly how many workers he will need or how much employment he will give.

Hence, in the so-called free labor market, no one knows what the reserve of labor should be for the next season or the coming year.

This uncertainty is supposed to be one of the advantages of competitive industry because it makes of competition something of a handicap game. Each employer gets what he can when he can, and each worker is expected to do likewise — if he can. And industries and workers that migrate from place to place only increase the amount of uncertainty.

To illustrate, we may ask how much reserve labor is needed for the textile industry? What labor is needed in the different branches of the industry? How does labor demand in the southern states vary from northern states? What should be the seasoned surplus of labor in the coal industry? How do these demands compare with those of the building industry? Should the percentage of unemployed be greater for skilled than for unskilled workers, or for women workers than for men?

In reality, then, the so-called pool of reserve labor is really a number of pools as varied and complex as the stock of goods in a department store. It offers no safe basis for determining how much unemployment is just enough for the "good" of business. Private industry, that does not want the laws of supply and demand to operate in relation to prices and production, is perfectly willing to let the regulation of wages and hours of work be guided by chance. But the laws of chance are ruthless, and too costly for the average worker. It is precisely because workers hold no aces in reserve that the big industrialists want to gamble with them in the open labor market. When the big industrialists gamble against one another they favor having rules for the game.

LESS LABOR AND MORE MACHINES

How, for example, could the problem of seasonal beet labor be met by the introduction of control? Each season the sugar companies want WPA projects discontinued because they interfere with the labor supply. Worker groups claim that if public work is suspended, the sugar processors will induce farmers to pay less for labor. At the end of the season the workers find themselves without money and the farmers find they have gained little or nothing. The sugar companies, on the other hand, usually fare well. But if workers and farmers received adequate compensation, beet sugar production, which is an uneconomic industry, might be crowded out of existence.

The beet sugar industry survives because it is subsidized by public money. It is protected, first, by a high tariff to keep prices of sugar up. The sugar companies obtain the high tariff by telling Congress it is necessary to protect the living standards of American workers. In practice, however, the companies, in order to show a profit, must depend upon wholesale exploitation of labor at substandard wages.

At the production end the beet sugar industry is also protected, because the workers who do not make a living wage turn to public relief for supplementary subsistence or, when they are fired, seek work from the federal government. Thus the industry is more nearly on a federal dole than are the workers, who at least earn part of their livelihood producing the sugar.

The beet sugar industry is only one of many that would oppose any effective regulation of the labor market. Private industries want a market such as they enjoyed before 1929, when there was unemployment but no work relief. Industrialists like to point out that in those days labor was self-sufficient. They argue, therefore, that if nothing is done, things will drift back to where they were in the "good old days."

The unemployed today are the same who would have scorned public aid prior to 1929, but industry is not the same. Industry is not in the business of making jobs but of curtailing them. It is doing less pioneering and more digging in. Instead of creating new work opportunities, industry has learned how to increase production with less labor and more machines. The effect on unemployment has been obvious. Too few workers have been taken out of

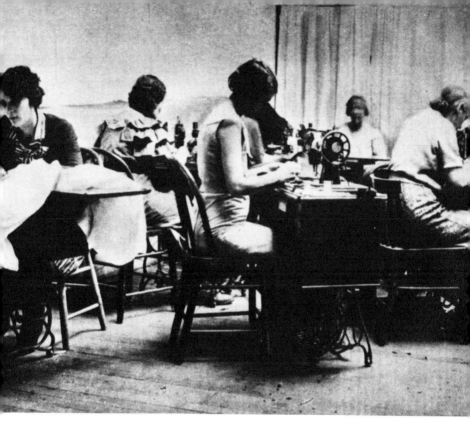

A sewing project in Idaho. In all states and in almost all counties, 220,000 women have been employed on WPA sewing projects. In two years these workers have produced for distribution through local relief agencies 108,400,000 garments, including dresses, shirts, jackets, and children's clothing.

A canning project in Vermont. WPA has built 746 canning units in 46 states. In some states the canning unit is operated as a project and the product is given to relief. In most places the unit is a community property which the people, singly or in groups, take turns using.

WPA household-aid worker in Boston takes the place of an ill mother. Housekeeping-aid projects have given employment to 12,000 women and have served 518,000 families. These workers visit the homes of the needy to care for the children, put the house in order, and do other necessary work in the event of infirmity, illness, or death.

WPA nursery school in Ohio. Mothers working on
WPA projects or other working mothers may leave
their small children in the nursery. WPA maintains more than a thousand nurseries.

Throughout the country 128,000,000 lunches are served daily to undernourished children. The food is provided by the local communities. WPA furnishes the labor on these projects. The school lunch program gives employment to 10,500 women from the relief rolls.

NYA recreational project in a Chinese mission, San
Francisco. This phase of the WPA program has
given employment to 40,000. In part the program
is responsible for the construction of playgrounds,
sport fields, swimming pools; and in part for the
supervision of these facilities in the local or state
parks, the national parks, and institutions.

Forty thousand pieces of glazed tile were used in this mosaic prepared for the Long Beach, California, Municipal Auditorium. Under the CWA program the federal government provided work projects for unemployed artists. This program was expanded under WPA. Five thousand artists have been employed on creative work or in teaching and research. More than 800 murals have been placed in public buildings.

Part of a mural in the courthouse of Morristown,
New Jersey. WPA is returning art to the people.
Fifty-four hundred murals and paintings have been
placed in schools and other public buildings. In
addition to oil paintings, 35,000 prints and 300,000
photographs, map drawings, and other art pieces
have been produced.

"The Role of the Immigrant in the Industrial Development of America," a mural being painted on the walls of a federal building at Ellis Island by WPA painters.

Children of Buffalo, New York, watching "Rip Van-Winkle," a puppet show. This is the most popular and least expensive type of children's theatre.

Archaeological "boondoggling." WPA workers
uncovering burials in an ancient mound. Scientists
have found that relief workers can be trained to
do the careful, patient digging required to un-
earth the hidden record of earlier American civil-
izations. Archaeological projects have discovered
materials which add invaluably to our store of
knowledge about extinct peoples.

WPA actors in "It Can't Happen Here." The play opened on the same night in 21 cities with 28 casts; it played 780 performances to 327,000 admissions. The Federal Theatre Project has played to a total audience of 27,000,000 in 27 states. A good portion of the admissions were people who cannot afford to attend private legitimate theatres. Fifty-two actors from the casts of "It Can't Happen Here" were released for private jobs.

Cast of "Macbeth," one of the most popular WPA plays. These actors played 116 performances in New York City, Chicago, Dallas, Detroit, Cleveland, and Indianapolis to an aggregate audience of 97,000. The Federal Theatre has reached many small cities where the legitimate private theatre has almost ceased to function.

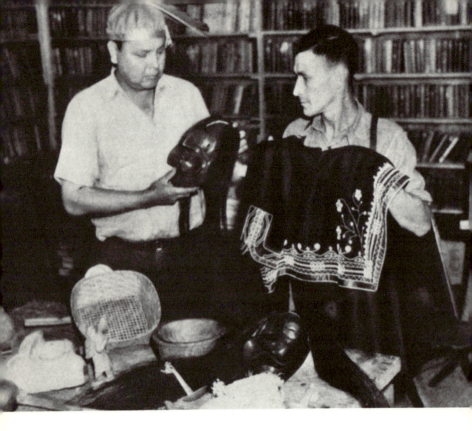

Two Seneca Indians assembling a collection of
ancient masks, war clubs, bowls, beaded shirts, etc.,
for museums. Indians may also be unemployed.

Lincoln House at Lincoln Village, Rockport, Indiana. WPA, through the historical American buildings survey, has made available pictures and drawings of 2,300 early buildings. Some of these have been reconstructed as public museums.

Diorama of Grand Rapids, Michigan, in 1827.
Miniature reproductions of buildings and historic
scenes represent a new type of architectural art
being developed by WPA.

the reserve labor pool, while other millions, with no personal reserves to fall back on are forced to hang on to uncertain part-time jobs.

The government, in its program of relief and work relief, has tried to restore some security to the unemployed worker, and in doing so has earned the enmity of those employers, big and small, who would prefer to continue as before.

When millions are unemployed, private industry can afford to be more selective in hiring workers. Only the top few are chosen, because industry wants the healthiest, the best trained, and the most energetic. Private industry wants only the bright, strong workers between the ages of eighteen and forty. The older, the slower, and the less efficient workers have to wait longer for jobs; many of them have no chance at all.

SOCIAL RATHER THAN PROFIT MOTIVES

The federal work program serves mainly the middle group between the most employable workers at the top and the least employable at the bottom of the reserve labor pool. The government assures private employers that it will give temporary jobs to these workers, but only until industry can re-hire them. Yet when private employers are urged to use such labor they protest: "We can't use relief labor. It has been spoiled by the dole or public work." Or: "We would hire this labor but these workers prefer to stay on relief."

It does not matter that in the executive and directorial strata of all businesses, incompetence and inefficiency are widespread. Only in the production branches does business insist on the maximum of skill, speed, and efficiency. Private employers cannot afford to hire any but first-class workers that can make a profit for them, nor can they afford to retain workers when there is no longer a profit to be made from their services. As private enterprise operates, such practices are normal and legitimate. Employers could not survive otherwise.

The government as an employer of labor is not bound by the restrictions of competitive enterprise. It can, therefore, assume the larger responsibilities that private employers cannot or will not assume. The government is guided by social rather than profit motivations. This in itself introduces a contradiction. Can government provide work for the unemployed, having their welfare in mind, and at the same time respect the demands of employers for a free labor market?

Can the government give a little work to some of the idle workers in the labor reserve and resist the pleas of the others? Employers profess to be fearful lest assumption of a little federal responsibility lead to more, and that more responsibility may lead to new efforts on the part of the government to regulate the labor market.

If unemployment continues unabated there may be good reason for such fears. A democratic government cannot long evade the responsibilities inherent in a democracy. If pressed to it by popular demand, democratic government may arrive at the point of resisting the doctrine of a *laissez faire* labor market. Democratic governments are slow to assume such responsibilities, but once having assumed them, they are slower in giving them up.

TAMING WILD HORSES

Under the outlawed NRA the government attempted to regulate the labor market with a view to increasing work opportunities. The suppression of child labor alone made thousands of openings for adult workers. The forty-hour week spread work. But since the abandonment of NRA many industries have gone back to forty-four hours, some to fifty-four and even to seventy hours, with a consequent lowering of wages per hour and a corresponding decrease in earnings and in the number of employed workers. Longer hours generally mean more profits for industry. They also mean more workers on the relief rolls, more unemployed living by work relief, and a consequent diminution of the total national income.

Under the old order of things the government had no more interest in regulating the labor reserve than it had in regulating that other wild horse of business, the stock market. We have seen the financial community subjected to regulation for the general good. We know, too, that the government can sponsor public power plants and cooperative transmission lines in order to force down the high rates for electricity. In order to guarantee to every citizen the right to work the government may eventually have to regulate the labor market as well.

Federal emergency relief has already, to a limited extent, operated as a regulatory factor in the labor market. And WPA, as the biggest single employer of labor in the United States, might easily become the arbiter of the minimum wage and of working conditions in private employment. No other public agency is in such a powerful position. Through WPA the government can purchase surplus labor just as, through other departments, it can buy surplus commodities.

Employers and economists who doubt the government's capacity to regulate the labor market would do well to study the emergency work agencies. Perhaps the day has already passed when the reserve pool of labor can be left to seek its own economic salvation. If that be true, future economic crises may assume a different form.

Employers had a chance to regulate their own labor problems under the NRA, but they fought effective regulation in any form. They still have the opportunity, but they cannot or will not take it. Imagine, for example, coal, steel, oil, and electric power cooperating, each industry with the other, to give labor a fair deal!

But in default of employer cooperation labor itself promises to become a factor in bringing about regulation from within, through the collective action of the workers. Unionization would tend to shorten hours and otherwise increase employment. Organization would also remove the fear that so many trained workers have, of being eliminated by industry after they have reached a certain age. In time, unionization should bring about such an equitable balance between wages and profits that workers would no longer be compelled to seek relief or work relief.

INVADING THE LUSH PRESERVES

The more sound regulation that can be injected into employment relations, the more secure will be the workers who still have jobs. Regulation cannot, of course, help the millions of relief workers who have already been rejected by industry. For a long time to come, whatever may be achieved in labor organization and labor market regulation, there will be many more workers than jobs. Even the most humane and just employers, in business to make money, cannot be expected to create jobs because workers need them.

This today is the function of government. Every state can find plenty of work that needs to be done. Instead of using two million man-years of labor during the next twelve months, the government could easily use ten million man-years, and there would still be work deficiencies. At that rate the labor pool would be emptied in three months.

If, then, public work to prevent unwanted idleness becomes a regular federal function, we may achieve a new relationship between government and the labor market in which the unemployed on public work will be the actual pool of reserve labor to which a controlled industry will apply for workers.

But the New Deal Administration seems to have no such intention of invading the lush preserve of private enterprise. Even the general public would probably not tolerate that much "invasion." American business, "generally apprehensive of the New Deal, and frequently hostile to it," is not without outside support in its criticism. Many workers, although not overly secure in their own job tenure, have so little comprehension of their best economic interests that they feel about regulation much as business does.

Other groups of workers, especially the chronically unemployed, want more regulation of industry and more public work. They have sent thousands of letters and telegrams to Congress and the President demanding that the WPA program be expanded rather than curtailed. Those who have given the problem any serious thought are coming to realize that public work relief cannot be terminated so long as there is unemployment, and that in time government regulation of the labor market is likely to be more, rather than less, effective.

VIII. A GOOD DAY'S WORK

CAN THEY DO A GOOD DAY'S WORK?

In a small Michigan community lives a man who is now fifty years old. An experienced mechanic, he makes most of his living doing odd jobs about town. From time to time he has been forced to apply for relief and has been assigned to WPA projects.

More than thirty years ago this man left his home town and went to Grand Rapids where he worked in a furniture factory. He later went West and worked on railroad construction. He worked four years as a railroad fireman. He worked in a foundry long enough to learn the moulder's trade. He went to Detroit and worked several years in the automobile plants, holding various skilled jobs.

In 1932 he was laid off. It was a general layoff this time; he had survived several earlier reductions of the force. He stayed in Detroit and tried for several months to get another job. There was no question about his ability or his industry. It was his age. He was forty-five then and was told he could not keep the pace. He finally left Detroit and came back to his home town.

Today this worker speaks of himself as an old man, although he is in good physical condition and has proved himself an efficient and versatile worker. In his home town he has worked as a painter. He drilled a well for a neighbor. As a mason, he erected a stone wall. He built a brick fireplace and several chimneys. He has repaired many roofs. He did the plumbing in a remodeled home. In the town garage he gets work occasionally as an auto mechanic.

But because he doesn't have steady work he has had to ask for relief.

From that same town in Michigan came a young woman who had had no work experience at all. She was a married woman with two small children. When her husband, who had never been a very good provider, deserted her, she thought she could find employment if she went to Chicago. She did get occasional jobs as a domestic, but they didn't pay enough to support her children. In the homes where she worked the children were not wanted.

Confident that in the West she could find work, she boarded her children with a private family and started in an old Ford car for California. She had counted on getting work along the way, but that was 1932 and there was no work. Her car broke down and she found herself adrift with a party of transients. In that company she continued on her way, riding the freight trains. She never reached California, but stopped in Arizona where she got employment as a cleaning woman in an auto camp.

After working several months without getting enough to pay for the support of her children, she resolved to return East. Again she traveled on the freight trains. In desperation, unable to pay their board bill, she stole the two little boys and again started on the road. She hitchhiked part way, but on most of the journey back to Arizona she and the children rode the freight trains, begging food from welfare agencies or from private citizens.

Working in the auto camp as a scrubwoman, and getting some help from local welfare agencies, this woman has lived for four years in Arizona. She has managed to keep the boys in school every year, and now one lad is a superior student in second year high school. For a year she has been working on WPA.

Of these two cases — and they are not exceptional — it can be said that though both are willing and capable, this man and woman are marginal workers. One has been forced out by private industry and the other could never get in. Neither wants to be on relief, but both have been forced to it by necessity. Both have had work on WPA and both would rather be on WPA than on the relief rolls. In each of these cases we have the same problem: if these workers cannot meet the stringent requirements for work in private industry, what test should they be required to meet on relief work?

To this question there is an individualist answer that recalls the Wayland book written in 1840. Concerning the man excluded from industry the answer would be: "In the competitive labor market workers try to get the best jobs they are able to hold. Employers try to get the best workers. The man made the proper adjustment. When he was forced out of one field of work he found a place in another field."

In the case of the woman the answer would probably be: "She should have stayed in her home community where she was known and forced her husband by law to support her children."

The trouble with such answers is that they fail to answer. The facts are that the man could not make an adequate living doing odd jobs and that the woman was driven from home by necessity. The answer for them is work, but there are millions of willing workers like these, who cannot find enough work and whose potential labor is going to waste.

THE KILLING PACE

Occupationally, the unemployed represent all crafts and skills, the good workers and the bad, the most efficient and the least efficient. Many of them could not qualify for private work because they are old, but they are not, as a rule, lazy. Many are young and untrained, but lack of training is not a mark of laziness; industry will not hire inexperienced workers if trained ones are available. Many unemployed workers are in some way handicapped, and not a few of them acquired their handicaps in private employment; yet private employers do not want them now. These varied types of rejected, untrained, or unwanted workers could not produce at a profit.

But is the test of profit the only test? What we need to discover now is whether there is not another standard which can be applied in employing those that cannot meet the profit test. Otherwise, to the extent that rejected workers fail to meet the prevailing standards of private industry, they will lose self-respect and personal dignity through idleness and the community will lose as well the benefit of their labor.

We can concede lower efficiency among certain types of unemployed workers without defending inefficiency; age, ill health, and malnutrition are frequently contributing causes. And without denying the validity of the profit test for private industry, we can still deny that the same test need be applied to all workers on public projects. Other considerations must be taken into account. Efficiency in private work will be as rigid as private industry can make it, but in relief work it must be relative.

Perry A. Fellows, assistant chief engineer of WPA, in an address before the Washington chapter of the Society for the Advancement of Management, compared the idea of efficiency in private industry with the social use of the term in public work. He said:

"Up to this decade the profit motive for work in America has so perfected the means for producing the goods and comforts which we all cherish that it is not strange if many people forget the existence of any other significant motive for human endeavors; and within its own realm of operations, the profit motive has set up standards of achievement so logical and widely accepted that it is all too easy to make the mistake of attempting to apply such standards where they cannot rightly be applied.

"This is one of the difficulties which we face, not only in the execution of our federal work program, but in the very formation of it. We are from first to last judged by many people having the point of view to which the profit ideal is the supreme criterion. These critics are not necessarily any more selfish than any of the rest of us; they may be, personally, generous and philanthropic, but they have not conceived of the federal work program as a kind of large socio-economic endeavor to which their familiar profit standards cannot at all points be correctly applied.

"The word 'efficiency' is a term in which many familiar profit standards are customarily summed up. It is supposed to connote the best way of doing things. Actually, it may mean only the best way of doing things for private profit. Instances can be found, without searching very hard, in which a private profit involves a public loss. Social bookkeeping includes items on its balance sheet which do not appear in private ledgers."

We need not look far to find examples of profitable jobs in private industry resulting in social loss and even havoc. An occasional case, if it is shocking enough, may get national attention. Newspaper readers will recall the circumstances under which several women in New Jersey lost their lives painting radium watch dials. The press reported the pitiable condition of the doomed women and their reasons for bringing suit against the watch company.

A social loss accompanies the operation of mines in which the workers are exposed to silicosis from breathing the glassy silica dust while operating power drills. At Delemar, Nevada, some years ago, there was a mill where precious metals were taken from the ore through a "dry process," by which the ore was crushed to a fine powder. It was, commercially, the most profitable method, but dozens of strong men, who thought they could withstand it, died from the dread silicosis.

The profitable operation of industry brings with it other social consequences beside personal hazards, which can be reduced, although usually not without a certain sacrifice of profits. There are, for example, many streams that have been polluted by industrial wastes dumped into the waters. The fish in those streams have been destroyed and wild life has been driven away. In countless cities and towns throughout the country the smoke and fumes from industrial plants have destroyed vegetation and undermined the health of people for miles around. Invariably these industries are very efficient in producing profits.

In this discussion, however, we are concerned only with the social losses that may accompany industrial efficiency when it is measured by the profit standard. These are social losses that can be directly attributed to the killing pace that all workers must maintain and from the physical deterioration that accompanies certain industrial profitmaking processes.

THE EMPLOYER'S TAX BILL

Suppose we apply the profit test to all workers and follow it to its logical conclusion; what will be the consequence to the millions unable to meet it? Workers may be worn down, crippled, or broken in health to the point that the industries they once served can no longer use them at a profit. From then on the social loss begins, unless other occupations can be found for these partially incapacitated workers.

Many persons rejected by industry will find some other employment, as did the man in Michigan, but in the process they may be obliged to reduce their living standards. Some of the rejected or technologically displaced workers may even find other private employment if they are given opportunities for re-training. But re-training would not solve the problem of the former Detroit automobile worker. He has training, but he doesn't have speed. Younger workers, not competing under the handicap of age, would have a far better chance of finding jobs if they were trained.

It is possible that the question of training by federal work relief agencies may come under discussion during coming months. It is a problem in which the older craft unions have a considerable stake, and so they may offer stubborn resistance to any federal training program. This proprietary, semi-vested interest of craft unions in skill is closely associated with the profit test.

Those who oppose training as part of the federal work program would do well to realize that project work does not offer very extensive training opportunities. A few skills might be taught adequately, but for others the possibilities on public work, particularly through such agencies as CCC and WPA, are limited. The most they could provide would be a pre-training service.

In the course of his work on CCC or WPA, if a youth is transferred from one kind of occupation to another and permitted to use different tools in different situations, he will acquire general work ability. In no small degree WPA and CCC have already enabled many young workers to get experience in handling tools, in the organization of work, in the care and use of materials, and in "teaming up" with other workers. Such pre-training experience as a substitute for apprenticeship would be amply justified if it did no more than give a youth the opportunity to review a few occupations before making a choice.

So far, however, pre-training has been incidental to, rather than integrated with other objectives. It cannot, in the final analysis, compensate for the social losses created by a ruthless application of the profit test. For other workers than the young, the work relief program might be likened to an industrial ambulance service that removes the casualties of industry, especially in the mill towns where the speed-up system, called the "stretch-out," prevails.

Under the stretch-out system, each worker is given all the work he can possibly do to the limit of his endurance, and the pace of all is set by the fastest. It is a good method for making profits, but it is hard on human beings. The money it makes for employers is more than offset by eventual social losses in the number of workers prematurely worn out. Some mill hands last a long time; others drop out very soon.

The factory or mill worker who has reached the end of his usefulness with one enterprise is not likely to be employed by another where the same profit test is applied to his output. And if he cannot find the same kind of work he must turn to other fields. Then, if he is not accepted, he must ask for public work or be content with the dole. Re-training him is a remote possibility.

The fierce competitive pace does two things. It eliminates those workers that cannot maintain it and sets the standard for hiring others. It serves as the measuring rod for putting some workers out and for keeping others from getting in. It undoubtedly makes money, but it as surely destroys workers.

Legally, the employer has no responsibility to his workers, either to those who are coming to the end of their usefulness or to those waiting outside for jobs. But in the long run, the social loss will appear on the employer's tax bill, and when it does he may be expected to join the chorus of those who call the unemployed lazy.

"NO RELIEF-BUMS NEED APPLY"

What will be the social effect on three or four million workers as they come to realize that they can expect little in the way of employment from private enterprise? Will the realization that they have been excluded or rejected by the labor market, except for very marginal work, stir them to concerted action? What effect will their exclusion have upon the behavior of other people toward them? Already the leaders of the unemployed are saying: "They are pushing us aside as if we were a caste of untouchables."

It is a fact that workers who accept relief are treated as if they were undesirables. Employers frequently refuse to hire workers who have been on the relief rolls. In a Montana newspaper an advertisement for workers closed with: "No relief bums need apply." In May, 1937, a Missouri businessman wrote to protest against additional appropriations for relief on the ground that workers on relief were not willing to take jobs in private industry.

Investigation disclosed that the gentleman from Missouri operated a lumber camp in the Ozarks in a region where the timber was so sparse that the most competent choppers could not make a living. Inquiry revealed, further, that he would not hire any workers if they had previously been employed on WPA, although he had been several times a successful bidder on government contracts. In an interview the protesting gentleman admitted he was not only against WPA, but that he opposed Social Security, the new banking laws, bank deposit insurance, and the income tax.

Such employer attitudes are bound to have their effect, and the more general they become the more will the unemployed be isolated and ostracized. Yet, although excluded by the efficiency cult and the profit test, they are still potentially useful members of society. A truly democratic government cannot push them aside, and if the burden of finding employment for them falls on government a substantial share of the cost will have to be saddled on the same recalcitrant employers who say: "No relief bums need apply."

The fundamental incentives of the profit test are negative. It survives on fear — fear of wage cuts, layoffs, demotion, or discharge. For industrial workers the chief incentive is insecurity. And because of this everpresent sense of insecurity, workers who have jobs tend to pit themselves against workers who do not. For the same reason unemployed workers who have not been reduced to the level of relief are pitted against the workers who are on relief. These are among the by-products of competitive enterprise in which employers struggle for profits and workers struggle for jobs.

Such jungle relationships between workers and employers, like those between classes of workers, are the natural consequences of unregulated competition in a situation where available jobs are far outnumbered by available workers. These are the negative costs of too much emphasis on the profit test.

What standards should be established for the surplus workers who can get little private employment or none at all? If public work is provided for them, by what methods should they be supervised in order to obtain from them the maximum of efficiency and work integrity? Is it possible to employ the jobless on public work without using the incentive of insecurity?

WORKERS LIKE TO WORK

Except as workers are encouraged to seek private employment, work relief is free of negative incentives. Lacking the profit motive, other means must be found for encouraging habits of industry. To instil work integrity in the unemployed on relief projects, it is essential to create work incentives to take the place of insecurity.

It should not be necessary to keep workers backed fearfully

against a psychological wall, as the stretch-out does. We need to bring about some more positive identification of the worker with his work, an identification that is lacking in private enterprise. The government work program for the unemployed must be a program for rehabilitating workers, enabling them to regain or to retain their self-respect.

In any public program dealing with many kinds of workers, the engineers find that the old production practices, aiming at low cost and high profits, cannot be applied. The new responsibility is not one of making goods to make money, but of fitting work to the workers. The engineers now have to maintain standards of efficiency and production, and at the same time to be mindful of the human side of employment.

Politically and theoretically, all men are created free and equal, but all men cannot attend with equal skill the same number of machines any more than they can bear equal tax burdens. It is possible, though, that the slow workers may be more useful at other tasks. Two workers, who may not be equal in productive capacity on the same kind of work when they sell their labor, must nevertheless pay the same price for bread. They may be equally efficient at a given task but not equally fast. The private employer cannot be concerned with adapting the slow worker, and so when the government undertakes to employ him it is committed to a more socially responsible approach.

We do not yet know how many new work incentives can be developed to replace fear and insecurity. A way has to be found to stimulate in the ditch digger the same personal interest in his work that an artist displays. We already know from work relief experience that it is not an impossible task. Workers on public jobs are keenly critical of inefficient methods, and when their complaints are adjusted they work with renewed interest, as though the road or building they were constructing belonged to them collectively. This feeling is native to workers, if the job situation can be arranged to develop it.

The most encouraging thing about the work integrity problem

is that normally the workers like to work. It is easy to arouse pride of workmanship whenever workers are given the opportunity to identify themselves with the products of their labor. The Paul Bunyan stories in the lumber industry bore witness to a pride of workmanship and production that died out when lumbering was mechanized and the work de-personalized. Luckily, one generation of industrial engineering has not been enough to rob the race of traits that have been in the human make-up for thousands of years.

This, then, is the problem we must solve — to revive the craftsmanship incentive that has been smothered by the routine of mechanized industry and by the profit test. It is easy to maintain work integrity on jobs where men use their tools. In practically all crafts there is bound to be a pride of workmanship and an instinctive striving for efficiency. It may be possible to elevate these psychological drives to the level they occupied in days not long past, when drilling contests, wood sawing contests, corn shucking races, beef butchering contests, and steer roping contests were the chief events at holiday celebrations.

If workers on public projects are shovel leaners, it only means that something is wrong with the work or with the supervision. Loafing and inefficiency, although they exist in ever-lessening degree, cannot and will not be defended. Happily, on public projects today there tends to be a higher degree of work integrity and a growing pride in the job. Integrity, we have learned, can be achieved without either the poverty bogey or the job pacing set by the fastest worker. It grows out of the interested, intelligent participation of each worker according to his ability. If we can inspire work integrity that is self-motivated we shall have come a long way from the profitmaking pace that can only be negatively stimulated through fear.

IX. WORK RELIEF AND THE PRESSURE GROUPS

THEY CALL IT "HEAT" IN WASHINGTON

Today all sections of the country look to Washington. More things are happening in Washington today than ever before — things that concern more people. It is only natural, therefore, that interested groups and interested individuals should bring the utmost pressure to bear on those who are in a position to influence the direction of legislation or the bestowing of government benefits.

In Washington such pressure is called "heat." Pressure groups that either oppose or favor a proposal before Congress put "heat" on the Congress, on the President, on department heads. They apply it most unrelentingly to administrative officials charged with executing the acts of Congress. And surely no recent activity of the federal government, no phase of the recovery program, concerns more people or has been subjected to more "heat" than the administration of relief.

In one way or another unemployment relief concerns people at all economic levels — employers, shopkeepers, workers on jobs, workers without jobs, even people that do not have to work. A great many of them are afraid that relief will increase their tax bills. Some see it interfering with their labor supply; others regard it as a threat to their wage scales; a few are genuinely disturbed about the moral implications of relief. But the unemployed are concerned only with getting jobs.

Some groups apply "heat" because they have something to sell. They want to unload on the government their supplies of steel, cement, lumber, machinery. Some favor public work if they can rent their equipment, sell insurance, dispose of textiles for sewing rooms, or obtain contracts for federal projects. Pressure groups may even insist on certain demands in one situation and on contrary demands in another.

Such a multitude of conflicting claims is the legitimate and inevitable consequence of a government spending-program. These demands and counter demands merely reflect the self-interest of the many groups and individuals that are bent on getting public benefits while benefits are available.

The collecting and spending of public money inevitably raises a two-way problem; it involves the people from whom the money is collected and those on whom it is expended. But no money collected and spent for any government function creates more discussion or arouses more antagonism than the money collected and spent for unemployment relief.

"IT IS MY PRIVILEGE TO DODGE" . . .

Not long ago Mr. J. P. Morgan spoke his mind on the charge, made by the President, that men of wealth use unfair devices to escape taxation. Mr. Morgan, who has not been entirely innocent of tax avoidance, was completely nonchalant about the matter. He said, in effect, that the man who paid taxes he could sidestep was downright foolish. Stated baldly, his attitude toward the government was: "It is my privilege to dodge, and yours to catch me if you can."

Citizens of Mr. Morgan's economic status are the leaders of the pressure groups that have had most to say about the burden of unemployment relief on the taxpayer. They are the sponsors of various associations that strive to keep relief appropriations at the lowest possible level. During the past year or more they have been sedulously promoting the idea that relief should be locally administered. Local relief, they claim, is more efficient and more humane. They could add, if they would, that the cost of local relief would then be saddled on the local residents, the middle class, and the poor, and not on the wealthy congregated in the money-centers.

The same taxpayer groups have been active in creating public sentiment for the sales tax, which is always a tax on consumption. So successful have they been that sales tax laws are in effect in more than twenty states and in a few cities. As a method of shouldering on the poor the burden of caring for the poor, the sales tax is unparalleled.

At intervals since the inception of federal relief and work relief, tax leagues have advocated that since workers who accept relief are really paupers they should not be permitted to vote. As yet, however, they have not attempted to pass a law disfranchising relief clients.

Rarely are the taxpayer pressure groups organized by small taxpayers, who, if they make complaints, are more likely to write as individuals. For example, one citizen wrote: "This money should not be spent to give work to aliens and communists. I am writing as a taxpayer." And an employer protested: "We taxpayers don't believe that the Government meant to give work to people who will not take private employment. WPA projects should be closed until the crops have been harvested."

SKILLFUL FLAG WAVING

Often the pressure group that specializes in "patriotism" can, by skillful flag waving, arrive at objectives not too closely identified with patriotism. This observation applies mainly to that species known as the professional flag waver or patriot. The professional can usually be distinguished by his skill in waving the flag with one hand while serving some selfish interest with the other.

Patriotic groups that have concentrated on the relief issue have been most successful in getting attention. They delight in "pointing with alarm" to: (1) The burden of relief on the taxpayer; (2) The danger of communists and other radicals using the relief program to overthrow the government; (3) The tendency of relief rolls and also work rolls to be filled with aliens; and (4) The demoralizing effects of the dole (in which they include work relief) on the morale of the American workers.

It is not easy to say who these "patriots" are, because so few are willing to identify themselves. We do know that most of the American soldiers who fought in the World War were recruited from the same economic classes that the relief workers come from today. Veterans' organizations know this, too, and have fought persistently for veterans' preference in certification for relief and in the assignment of workers from relief rolls to WPA projects.

Veterans' organizations have agitated unremittingly for the exclusion of aliens from relief and work rolls so that more benefits could be given to citizens — and to veterans before all others. After four years of incessant struggle against the distribution of unemployment benefits on the basis of need only, these pressure groups succeeded in having the exclusion of aliens and veterans' preference written into the Emergency Relief Appropriation Act of 1937.

In the early years of the depression the same patriotic pressure groups managed to get a drive started to deport aliens. A number of indigent aliens, illegally in the country, were actually deported. Others, legally here, were offered free passage home. Pressure groups would have the government consider any alien on relief an undesirable pauper and subject to deportation. But that would mean the breaking up of 100,000 or more families of which the husband or wife is a citizen, and would gratuitously penalize more than 200,000 American-born dependents.

In considering the plight of the unemployed foreign born it is worth recalling that there was a time not long ago when this country welcomed a vast immigrant army every year. Agents of American companies scoured the cities of Southern and Eastern Europe in search of gullible workers. From steel mills, coal mines, factories came the demand for cheap, foreign labor — and plenty of it. The immigrant worker, unlike the native-born, asked for little, and on his strength and endurance much of American industry was built and expanded. Is he now to be regarded as an undesirable citizen, simply because the industries his labor developed no longer have any use for him?

As for the patriotism of the unemployed who receive relief or work benefits, this much can be said on the basis of four years of federal relief experience: (1) Most of these workers are good neighbors; (2) They are devoted to their families; (3) They are law-abiding members of their communities; and (4) They try to give the job a good day's work.

Leaders of patriotic groups in their attacks on New Deal unemployment relief too often act from questionable motives. Under cover of the relief issue they are really waging a major offensive against all phases of the New Deal.

DEFENDERS OF BIG JOBS

In another chapter we considered the influence of those pressure groups that favor big construction projects rather than the type of projects normally handled by WPA. The contractors that favor big jobs are represented by such powerful groups as the Associated General Contractors of America and the American Roadbuilders' Association. Like other organizations, they are eager to get new markets opened for durable goods. They like government contracts and are disturbed lest too much money be spent for relief appropriations and not enough for materials.

In Massachusetts, FERA sponsored a project for operating a knitting mill which had been idle for two years. The mill, one of three small industrial plants in the town, had formerly employed about a hundred workers. The other two plants, a paper mill and a machine shop, functioned only intermittently. The knitting mill was put into operation with about eighty unemployed workers, most of whom had held jobs there before.

Although operations were slow in starting, it was not long before the mill was producing outerwear knit goods of the highest quality at a cost under that of private production.

Other knitting mill owners, who had thought the mill could not be operated with relief labor, began to protest. And when the force at the mill had been increased to ninety workers and the production costs declined still further, the knitting mill proprietors swung into action.

Their protests were picked up by the press. Hundreds of newspapers in all parts of the country published sympathetic editorials. But not one explained that the local Chamber of Commerce favored the project. Upon investigation, Washington officials learned that the townsfolk in two public meetings had voted the funds to pay for light, heat, power, and rent. FERA paid the wages and supplied the raw materials from which thousands of sweaters were knitted and distributed to relief families.

When the mill owners were told that the project had received local approval and support, and that it was an efficient and useful undertaking, a representative of the industry said: "We don't care who is for it. We are against it."

The knitting industry, however, would have been glad to take government contracts to make goods, although it would not have felt obliged to give employment to the unemployed on relief. Certain individual mill owners, in fact, were not unwilling to rent their plants and equipment to the government. But collectively they were of another mind.

Members of the knitting industry behaved much as did the mattress makers. They said: "The government should not manufacture goods. That is our way of making a living. The government should buy from us."

Among the small merchants, though, a different attitude prevails. In the mill town just referred to the small storekeepers favored government operations because it brought to town a payroll where none had been for many months.

The knitting mill, which started as a state FERA project, was discontinued under WPA. Pressure against it was too great.

LABOR PRESSURE

It is no criticism of labor unions to describe them as specialized pressure groups. That they are is proof only that they have adjusted themselves to the ways of contemporary government. They could not otherwise survive against highly organized industry. Labor leaders have had experience with employer pressure groups; they have fought to gain ground and to hold it. If union workers are interested at all in the federal program for the jobless it is because they want to protect their hard-won standards and to obtain all possible new benefits.

According as they are able or not able to get public benefits, craft unions are likely to differ about the merits of WPA. The carpenters in a city may be in favor of a works project and the bricklayers against it; but each union within a month may have changed its position. The asbestos workers in an eastern city said in July, 1937: "WPA could go out as far as we are concerned. We never get jobs in our trade." The same union held the opposite opinion a month later because nineteen asbestos workers had been assigned to WPA.

It is not surprising that union men who have jobs should be interested in what the government does for the unemployed. They are as anxious to see standards and relief-work wages kept high as their employers are to have them kept low. The unions fear that low standards on public relief work may tempt private employers to "worsen" conditions for all labor. On this issue worker and employer groups are irreconcilable, and the government stands in the middle whenever the Works Program hires the unemployed and whatever the wage scale it sets.

The regular so-called "old line" craft unions are not opposed to the work relief program for the unemployed so long as the jobless are not put to work in competition with them. Bricklayers, carpenters, painters, engineers, or any other craft union workers, feel they have rights in the job jurisdictions for their crafts.

The local union not only claims the exclusive right to do a certain kind of work in a prescribed territory, but tries to control the number of persons who may learn the craft. The union, also, within its preëmpted territorial jurisdiction, tries to maintain a closed, or union, shop. These are a few of the difficulties the federal government encounters when it offers employment to relief workers in any craft over which a union claims control.

It is easy to understand why leaders of the old line unions owe their first loyalty to their dues-paying members and why they want to corner the good jobs. If there is a job shortage the non-union workers among the unemployed must look out for themselves. Employers who have contracts with unions feel the same way: they want their regular workers if they can get them. Not only are they reluctant to hire strangers, but they are especially unwilling to take any from the relief rolls. Left thus to their own devices, the unemployed have done the only thing possible for their protection — they have formed their own unions.

THE UNEMPLOYED ORGANIZE

During the first three depression years, before there was any federal relief or work relief, the unemployed did a great deal of demonstrating. They paraded in the big cities; they staged job marches to the city halls; they launched mass movements on Washington. There was plenty of activity, but none of it could have been called organizational in character. The people met, demonstrated as a crowd, and separated.

There was not even talk of unemployed unions in those direct relief and pre-relief years. Though some of the unemployed were members of trade unions, they had no organization of their own, paid no dues to anything, had no committees, no regular officials, and no regular scheduled meetings of which records were kept. All such evidences of unionism, insofar as they now exist, only appeared after the unemployed were put to work on public relief projects.

The "World Unemployment Day" demonstration of March 6, 1930, was a response to leadership; but it was not worker organization. Six years later, on April 7, 1936, the Workers Alliance of America convened in Washington. The 791 delegates from more than 200 towns and cities did not gather simply as mass marchers, but as spokesmen for groups of workers back home. They claimed to represent 300,000 active members of the Workers Alliance.

The delegates were not repulsed as were earlier job marchers on Washington. Instead, they were permitted to use the luxurious auditorium of the newly completed Department of Labor building. They made speeches, passed resolutions, sent committees to visit representatives of the Administration and Congress, and, having finished their business, went their way.

We mention the Workers Alliance because it is at present the only national organization of the unemployed and is now in its third year of existence. It tries to be a federating agency for all types of smaller unemployed groups in states and cities. Working from its headquarters in Washington, the Alliance concerns itself with putting pressure on Congress and on all administrative officials who have anything to do with work or relief. Affiliated with neither the American Federation of Labor nor the Committee for Industrial Organization, the Workers Alliance nevertheless strives to be on friendly and cooperative terms with both.

Not all unions or other local organizations of the unemployed are affiliated with the Workers Alliance. For example, Oklahoma has a strong statewide union, the Veterans of Industry of America; Pennsylvania has another, the Pennsylvania Security League. Both are outside the Alliance. The Veterans of Industry is expanding into neighboring states, where, as in Oklahoma, it aims to be a guiding factor in elections. Its membership includes not only employed and unemployed workers but the small farmers as well.

The Security League is made up largely of leaders of several Pennsylvania groups that are interested in relief, public work, and other welfare activities.

Although the Alliance claims to have in all its affiliated groups a dues-paying membership of 300,000 workers, nobody knows exactly what the aggregate is. But whatever its total membership, the Alliance claims to speak for *all* unemployed workers. It is prepared to advise all worker groups on when and how to exert pressure against the government to get greater relief appropriations. Its general objectives are few and simple. It encourages workers to join the Alliance or the old established unions to fight for union wages and improved working conditions, and to cooperate with unions in trying to gain these ends. It urges the unemployed not to take jobs as strikebreakers, but to support any unions that may be on strike.

Because the Administration is tolerant toward labor organization, public projects offer every inducement to unionization. With no ban against them, unemployed unions spring up quite spontaneously in any community, especially when workers feel they have grievances that need adjusting, when layoffs are threatened, or when the leaders of such groups believe that by organization they can obtain wage increases.

TACTICS OF UNIONS OF THE UNEMPLOYED

An example of spontaneous organization is the former National Unemployed Workers Protective League that was started by about thirty WPA workers in a middle western town. They elected officers, wrote a constitution, mimeographed handbills and got out a letterhead on which was printed the name of the union, its motto, and the names of officers. Next, a membership drive increased the NUWPL membership to about 120 out of the 500 WPA workers in the locality.

At their meetings League members passed resolutions setting forth specific grievances relating to low pay, shortage of projects, recent layoffs, adverse working conditions, and the arbitrary conduct of certain foremen. The statement of grievances was followed by written demands, copies of which were sent to local WPA officials, the mayor of the own, state, and federal WPA officials, the Secretary of Labor, and the President of the United States.

State and local WPA officials found upon investigation that many of the grievances were justified, but that some of the larger demands could not be met, particularly the demand for a twenty per cent wage increase. Not satisfied, the NUWPL called a strike, picketing all projects in an effort to persuade the rest of the relief workers to come out. The WPA offices were picketed, too, and committees were sent to the City Hall and the local Chamber of Commerce, demanding support for the strikers.

Thereupon certain other organizations in the town passed resolutions against the strikers, so that finally it became necessary to close the projects for a few days. That only served to arouse against the striking WPA workers the hostility of those who were temporarily laid off. After a few days the projects were re-opened and practically all of the strikers went back to work.

Several weeks later the union was reorganized, with new officers, a new letterhead and a new name — the WPA Defense Council. The officers presented a sweeping demand to the WPA. They wanted on each project job stewards who would represent all workers on the projects. They got a job steward on each project for those workers who wished to be represented by them, but WPA officials refused to require all workers to submit their complaints through the stewards.

The new union, the WPADC, has continued to function, although it has never attracted to its ranks more than twenty per cent of the relief workers. The active membership comprises less than five per cent of the relief workers in the community.

The tactics of unemployed groups do not differ greatly from one community to another. They pass resolutions, parade, throw picket lines around offices or projects and send delegations to wait on the officials in charge of relief or work relief. They usually concentrate their efforts on the government, although in some of the larger cities they have gone straight to employers and business groups demanding private jobs. On a number of occasions when business leaders have publicly declared that work does exist for those who will take it, they have been visited the next day by committees of the unemployed asking the whereabouts of the work.

THE UNEMPLOYED AND OTHER UNIONS

When the unemployed try to organize, they receive scant encouragement from any quarter. The pressure groups of industry and finance become panicky at the thought of unemployed unionism. They decry any unemployed activity as evidence of the spread of "communism," not realizing that very few of the unemployed have any knowledge of communism or any interest in it.

The attitude of conservative labor leaders toward unions of the unemployed is not essentially different. In a few localities the unemployed have received encouragement from the regular unions, but ordinarily the established craft unions are either indifferent to or skeptical of any organizational efforts on the part of the unemployed.

Regular old line unions are job-security business associations. The members expect to receive, through their union, work benefits to which they would not otherwise have access. If there is a building job to be had, the union bricklayers want the work; they are not likely to favor sharing it with bricklayers who may belong to a union of the unemployed.

Members of regular labor unions in good standing expect to be served first; they pay dues to insure their job priority. A union member too long out of work may fall behind in his dues and may lose his union standing in the same way that he would lose his insurance policy if he could not pay the premiums. When a job appears on the horizon, the union worker who has not paid up cannot step ahead of the union man who has. If the unemployed crowd in and the union workers are pushed out; if on WPA projects workers are assigned only on the basis of need and ability, it is easy to see why, on the work-relief issue, the regular unions sometimes line up on the side of businessmen. The unions of the unemployed are regarded as competitors by the more conservative unions.

The unemployed unions organize only in relation to relief work. On public jobs such as the big PWA projects, operated by contract, unions of the unemployed do not thrive. These jobs are under the control of the regular unions. The unemployed unions, to the extent that they exist, are found more often on the non-contract or force account type of public work used on the projects of WPA.

As far as objectives go, the aims of the unions of the unemployed are the same as those of other unions; they want plenty of work at good wages. They prefer private jobs, but if they cannot get them they demand public work. Like the members of other unions, they would rather work than be on relief.

Yet unemployed unionism differs from any other in several respects. It is cheaper; it embraces all crafts, all ages, and neither in theory nor in practice does it draw lines on sex, race, or religion. The unemployed union maintains no discipline and establishes no standards of work ability. It is, in fact, so loosely integrated that it almost ceases to be a union.

The unions of the unemployed also differ from regular unions in being much more militant in the tactics they employ. They are more catholic in their sympathies, too, as evidenced by their tolerance toward all workers. Their leaders are younger and perhaps more idealistic and zealous; for most of them, the job of organizing the unemployed is a labor of love. The money returns, when there are any, rarely exceed seven to ten dollars a week. Most of the organizers get nothing at all, in fact are usually money out of pocket.

Leaders of the unemployed tend to adopt all the concepts and even the terminology of the regular unions. They demand a union wage, collective bargaining, the closed shop. Unemployed workers who do not go out with them on "strike" are called "scabs" or strikebreakers. When sit-in and sit-down strikes broke out in private industry, the unemployed unions were quick to stage their own sit-in and sit-downs, although such extreme tactics have usually been confined to a few unions of white collar and professional workers in the larger cities, notably in New York.

THE UNEMPLOYED STAND ALONE

It was perhaps inevitable that in the current conflict between the AF of L and the CIO, the unions of the unemployed should become involved. With few exceptions, their sympathies and support have been extended to the CIO. This is especially true in Ohio and Michigan, where the tie-up between the two groups has been closer than anywhere else. Before the CIO issue arose, the Workers Alliance, on behalf of the unemployed unions, sought the cooperation of the AF of L. But what the future relationship of the unemployed unions to either the CIO or the AF of L will be is unpredictable.

Although unemployed groups are apt to have left-wing leanings, during the last presidential election they were encouraged in their pressure tactics in a number of states by right-wing politicians bent on embarrassing the New Deal Administration. These alliances proved to be not very happy ones, especially for the politicians who gave the leaders of the unemployed financial support which they could not afford to continue.

However difficult to understand their tactics may seem at times, these unemployed unions have rendered a real service to large numbers of workers. Not only have they been an educational force, but in discouraging strikebreaking by the unemployed they have stiffened the morale of regular union men in their struggle for union recognition and better working conditions in private industry. They have also served as a protection for individual workers on public relief projects. For no matter how hard the government may try to establish satisfactory labor relations, there will always be isolated cases of discrimination and favoritism on the part of some foremen and minor officials.

The unions of the unemployed can be and have been effective in obtaining equality of treatment on the job. To perform this protective function and to present the case for all the jobless are services that more than justify the existence of the unemployed unions.

As a pressure group the unemployed stand alone. Opposed to them are all the other pressure groups — the taxpayer leagues seeking special exemptions, the manufacturers in search of government contracts, industries clamoring for tariff protection, publishers wanting lower postage rates, contractors, and corrupt labor unions demanding big public projects which they can monopolize.

In pressing for their demands, most pressure groups are no less insistent than the unemployed; they are merely more subtle in their approach. Through their well-financed and socially acceptable lobbies they can get action because they have something to trade, whereas the unemployed, having nothing but their labor to offer, can only parade, write protests, and put their women and children in the picket line. One method is no less democratic than the other.

Every powerful interest in the country has its "representatives" or its "spokesmen" in Washington. Even the mayors of cities have a lobby, and states have their "ambassadors" at the capital. It is through these pressure groups, each putting on "heat" in its own way for its own interest, that democracy operates. Some pressure groups win out because they have money; others control public opinion through the press, the radio, or the screen. The unemployed have only their votes behind them, but these votes, if they are ever coordinated, may some day be able to command the things the jobless army wants — simply the right to work, the right to live.

X. WORK RELIEF AND THE
PROFESSIONAL

"POLITICS"

When, during the 1936 presidential campaign, the cry of "politics" was raised against the federal work relief program, WPA was the center of attack. That, of course, was to be expected, since WPA had on its rolls eight or ten times the number of workers on all other federal work rolls combined.

The term "political," when applied to a public activity, or to the activities of individuals in public life, frequently carries with it the implication of bad faith or corruption. In that sense the New Deal recovery program has been the least political enterprise ever sponsored by any government. Especially is this true of the work relief program.

Most states and communities are familiar with the political method of handling poor relief, and in many towns and counties the old ways still survive, despite their injustice and corruption. Federal direct relief, and later work relief, started out on a high plane, and federal supervision has kept them there. It is probably easier for the government, safely removed from the passions and loyalties of localities, to be at the same time more impersonal and more realistic.

If WPA is political at all it is because people are political, as

Cattle being shipped from the drought area of South Dakota. Millions of drought cattle were purchased by the federal government. Had they not been, the farmers in that dry region would have suffered a billion dollar loss.

Gully erosion on the Collins Game and Forest Reservation between the Tennessee and Cumberland Rivers in Kentucky. The public domain is the farm of the people. Millions of man-years of labor will be required to restore the land surface of Uncle Sam's neglected farm to the condition it was in when he took it from the Indians.

WPA workers planting seedlings in the St. Joe National Forest, Idaho. In 1936, under direction of the United States Forest Service, WPA and CCC planted 215,000,000 trees on 219,000 acres. An equal number were planted by the states and other federal agencies as part of the erosion control program. Our reforestation work is more than 30 years behind.

CCC boys in Virginia. Workers like these increased the wealth of the United States by a million man-years of labor. A few items to their credit are 37,000 small bridges in the national parks and forests; 3,000 miles of fencing; 13,000 public camp places with fire pits, running water, and comfort stations. They stocked streams and lakes for 200,000,000 fish. No estimate can be made of the value of CCC work in forest preservation and erosion control.

CCC boys making a road through the Lassen National Forest, California. CCC has built 85,000 miles of forest road and 20,000 miles of forest and mountain trail. These are defenses against forest fire. CCC has expended 4,000,000 man-days of labor fighting forest fires.

South Dakota farmers building a storage dam, working against a background of dust. This dam will back up 230 acres of water in a section where water *must* be conserved. Thousands of small dams have been constructed in the drought states by WPA and CCC; many were built under the FERA program.

A little storage dam in Kansas. With FERA and WPA funds several thousands small storage ponds have been constructed to hold back the water in those regions where too little rain falls. Equally important are the thousands of wells drilled by the government drought aid program.

Apache Dam in New Mexico, built by CCC to
control floods in the narrow canyons. CCC has
constructed 4,000 small impounding and diversion
dams, moving 22,000,000 cubic yards of earth and
rock.

Water for Denver brought over the Continental Divide in a sixty-two mile conduit built by PWA. For most of the way it flows through tunnels and syphons.

Bonneville Dam on the Columbia River near Portland, Oregon. On this project will be spent $32,-000,000 of PWA money. It is at once a flood control, erosion control, navigation and power development project. It will save its cost in cheap power to the Pacific Northwest.

Lock No. 7 (in Minnesota), one of several locks and dams built by Army engineers, on the Mississippi River. For this combined project PWA granted $100,000,000. For all rivers in the United States an expenditure of $5,000,000,000 could be made which would save far more than that in flood control, electric power, and aid to navigation projects. If the work is not done more than $5,000,000,000 will be lost.

Control shaft in one of the diversion tunnels of
the world's biggest earth-fill dam at Fort Peck,
Montana. It will convert the Missouri River into a
lake 175 miles long. Although started by contractors, the work will be finished by Army engineers,
thus offering a good opportunity to compare government efficiency on public work with that of private contractors. Fifty millions of PWA money
will be expended. This dam will control flood
waters which will be used for irrigation.

A Dust Bowl family moving to California. More than 200,000 farm families have been forced out on the roads in all parts of the United States. As a temporary service, the Resettlement Administration has established a number of wayside camps in which some migrants may find a temporary habitat while searching for work. What they really want is land to settle on.

Rehabilitation loan farmer in Arkansas. Resettlement Administration has extended rehabilitation loans to 460,000 farm families for necessities. The average loan was $360. It has also aided 54,000 farmers to reduce their debts from $175,000,000 to $130,000,000. Except where farmers can get work on WPA, most federal assistance extended to them is in the form of loans. To date, in spite of drought conditions, they have repaid 46 percent of these obligations.

Fairbury Farmsteads, Nebraska. One of 94 Resettlement Administration projects, of which 29, providing homes for 1,316 families, are completed, and 65 providing homes for 7,900 families are under construction. Tenants are privileged to lease these farms for periods of five years, or purchase them under a 40 year plan at an interest rate of 3 percent. Average size of individual farms at Fairbury Farmsteads is 19 acres.

Tygart Valley Homesteads, West Virginia. A Resettlement Administration project for the rehabilitation of 250 families of timber workers and miners.
The income of the farmers will be derived from
various cooperative agricultural enterprises now
under way. There are still several million underprivileged farm families in economic bondage.

people in a democracy should be. WPA has one hundred thousand foremen on its rolls. Another hundred thousand persons have more or less to do with selecting the workers, planning the projects, providing local contributions, or supervising the administration of WPA in their communities. Most of the people who are connected with WPA in administrative capacities are politically minded.

WPA could not function without the fullest cooperation of federal, state, and local political leaders, but it cannot, nevertheless, be managed by politicians for the usual political ends. In the first place, the work relief program is too openly administered. So many people are interested from so many points of view that it does not yield readily to the old time manipulation. Employers, labor unions, and the unions of the unemployed scrutinize the work with a critical eye. They are always asking questions, and if they are not satisfied with the answers they get locally, they write to Washington.

A second obstacle in the way of politicians who like to "get their feet in the trough," is that WPA is managed by a partnership control; it is both a federal and a local program. But the big difference between WPA and other types of local public work is that the local politicians do not handle the money. They neither pay the labor, buy materials, or rent equipment, nor do they set the standards for such expenditures. It is this difference that takes the WPA out of the old "pork barrel" category.

Furthermore, WPA is kept almost entirely free of political favoritism by the federal policy of using trained workers in administrative positions. This practice was begun with FERA and CWA, and has always been the standing tradition in other federal bureaus and departments.

When trained workers were brought in to administer FERA, the plan found little favor in many sections of the country. Special interests wanted the money given to the states, which would then dole it out to the local communities where the "people" would decide how it should be spent.

FERA did grant money to states, but federal officials followed the money to the spending points. The government took the position that even though the funds allocated by FERA technically became state funds, the people expected them to be spent under federal guidance and supervision. So it was that whenever things went wrong there was a general assumption that the fault lay with the federal government.

The FERA policy of using trained administrative personnel was continued by WPA. And if WPA has been threatened from time to time with political exploitation, the effects of it have been only temporary; because basically WPA operates on a strictly professional basis.

It is this professional opposition to "spoils politics" that frustrates the aims of people who fatten on the gleanings of politics. The professionals of the relief program are the "career" officials of the government, who are stronger in their technical and expert unity than any set of spoilsmen, and more enduring in their loyalty than any politician.

The word "expert" is used here only in its commonsense application. It implies effectiveness, efficiency, and integrity to work. It applies as much to the thoroughly competent file clerk as to an accountant who would quit his job rather than make a false report. Specifically, in relation to the Works Program, we have in mind the corps of engineers, social workers, labor officials, accountants, and other special workers.

"THE UNWARRANTED USE OF BRAINS"

A well-known publisher who would not think of running his newspaper with any but trained workers, declared in an editorial in 1933, "This unwarranted use of brains in government must stop."

This august ultimatum on the management of democratic government harks back to the days of Andrew Jackson when most right thinking people believed that any honest average citizen could administer any public office or hold any public job.

Long ago private industry got away from the notion that any worker could hold any job, and while the publisher just quoted may not have realized it, the government has been getting away from the notion, too.

The real work of the New Deal Administration is carried on by a corps of lesser officials, referred to in this chapter as "experts." They have had a great deal to do with carrying on the emergency program, and despite occasional local hostility they have successfully cooperated with political leaders in launching such programs as CWA. In less than a month CWA set up projects in thousands of communities and placed four million jobless workers on emergency payrolls. This feat could have been accomplished only by the hundreds of "experts" trained in the handling of work and people.

The "expert" is usually distinguished from the politician by his professional integrity. He takes pride in his work and is jealous of his reputation in his particular field. To the extent that the politician is different, it is due to his being in a different situation, for he, too, is a professional. His field is service to his constituents, upon which depends the security of his job, whether he be an Alderman, County Commissioner, Governor, or Congressman.

Contrary to popular belief, the saving trait of the politician is his preoccupation with people. His wish to be of service to his constituents is usually a genuine desire to do what he thinks people want done. If he swings from one side of an issue to another, it is more likely to mean that he has sensed a change of sentiment among his constituents, rather than that he has changed his own views.

Politicians are necessary functionaries in a democracy. They know more about the mechanics of government than the average citizen can ever know, and more about local needs and problems than the average citizen cares to know.

The local political worker, whatever his office, is forever beset with requests and demands from individuals and groups. His constituents expect him to help them get jobs; and if government rules stand in the way of their getting jobs, they expect the politician to alter the rules or to get exemption from them. To these many and varied demands for favors the politician cannot turn a deaf ear.

In his relation to the federal agencies, whether PWA, RFC, or WPA, the politician stands between the wants of the people and the rules of the program. He invariably finds the benefits available to him too limited for the local demand, and so he cannot avoid trying to get as many of them as he can for his constituents. In fact, if political leaders behaved in any other fashion there would be no need for a trained personnel in government service to meet relief issues on the basis of objective realities.

The best evidence we have that politicians have not captured control of the Works Program is the fact that there have been no bags of money passed around and few scandals, although billions of dollars have been expended through the agency of thousands of people, not a few of them professional politicians.

POLITICIANS MEET THE SOCIAL WORKERS

American political traditions were disturbed most when the federal government entrusted to trained social workers the task of expending relief funds.

The government called upon social workers because they constituted the only group that was in any way qualified to distribute relief in terms of professional requirements. They had received their training and experience in professional schools as well as with private agencies. And whatever the shortcomings of ordinary social work, the need for this type of training and experience was imperative when the federal government assumed responsibility for relief.

Social workers were first engaged when FERA was established to do a dole-dispensing job. At that time there was no thought of work relief except as local communities carried on their own. It was the social workers who got the federal unemployment relief program under way. With no precedents to guide them, without hustle or drum-beating, they perfected an administrative system that functioned. Slowly, since then, the unemployment program has evolved, changing form as it progressed, until it has finally become a program of work.

Social workers knew about people, but very little about work, certainly nothing about planning a work situation into which to fit the jobless. Most of them, having worked for private charities in the cities, had already encountered the unemployed. Unfortunately, they were used to dealing with unemployment in terms of the private charity bias and they brought with them into public service the traditional concepts about "worthy" people, sobriety, industry, patience, and gratitude. It was right, they felt, to believe that any worker who wanted a job could get it, and some social workers found it difficult to give up that idea when they encountered the unemployed in public service.

As for the jobless, many of them before they appealed for federal aid had been without work for from one to three years. They had suffered too much from local public relief and, before that, from private charity. They had acquired a dislike for charity which carried over to the local public dole and was later readily transferred to federal relief. Thus, for the unemployed, the social worker became the symbol of charity and relief, with all their despised and humiliating implications.

Social workers had never been expected to put people to work. They rarely did more in that respect than to establish woodyards which were so often used to administer the "work test" that determined whether a relief applicant was "worthy." Sometimes, though, they went so far as to put on drives through women's clubs to find odd jobs for the unemployed, jobs like fixing screens, cleaning basements, mowing lawns, shoveling snow, or raking leaves. Thus the social workers, through the private charities supported by the rich, were the original "boondogglers."

Although most social workers favored federal unemployment relief in 1933, few were qualified to plan a national program. Too

many of them still cherished the old-fashioned notions about unemployment. They believed, with the leaders of business, that the
existing social order was functioning well enough, and while ad-
mitting the volume of unemployment, they were unable to look
beyond the idle worker for the causes of his idleness. It has taken
some rapid and basic adjustments on the part of the social-work
profession to make the sudden transition from the private welfare
field wherein one point of view prevailed to the public field
wherein another had superseded it.

Imagine the shock it must have been for a social worker under
FERA to be asked to certify workers on strike. Formerly the social
worker would have said to the striker, "You had a job in the mill,
but you went on strike. Why don't you go back to your job in the
mill?" Even on WPA, in the few cases where work has been given
to strikers, there have been social workers who could not understand why aid should be given a worker who of his own volition
stays away from work.

Social workers frequently bring to public service certain attitudes which the politicians call "hard," but then, they would call
politicians irresponsible and sentimental. Social workers have, for
example, been slow to recognize that "reliefers" like to think of
themselves as workers; they show resistance to relief clients when
the latter insist on their rights as citizens.

In the final analyis, however, these "state-of-mind" obstacles to
social work in public relief are far outnumbered by other qualities,
not the least of which are professional integrity, industry and cour-
age. In a program committed to spending public money where it
is most needed, social work has been a bulwark against the demands for distribution of public relief on the basis of nepotism,
favoritism, or purchase through politics.

That systematic social work is becoming a permanent part of
the fabric of the Works Program can readily be seen in the rapidity
with which the new terminology of social work is being appropriated. Not only the workers who deal with the unemployed, but
the engineers, and even the politicians, use freely and with confi-

dence such expressions as "client," "interview," "contact," "plan," "psychosis," "clearance," "certification," "priority," "budget," etc.

ENGINEERS HAVE ALSO BEEN LEARNING

Many members of the engineering profession found as much difficulty as did social workers in adjusting themselves to the job of putting rejected labor to work. In their experience few engineers had ever encountered a responsibility quite like it. The profession had grown up much like social work, as an adjunct of industry. Engineers believed in a free labor market wherein workers competed for jobs as employers competed for business.

The human side of unemployment had never been an engineer's problem. In school and on the job the engineer learned about work and materials, about chemical and mechanical forces, about stresses and strains, how to make things and how to move them; but he learned very little about people.

In private industry engineers served their employers well; often they were the same employers who, by supporting private charitable agencies, helped pay the salaries of the social workers. Indirectly, through serving their employers, the engineers served society by making goods swiftly and cheaply. The process of making goods, however, was a means of making money.

Engineers perfected the automobile, enriching their employers and, incidentally, benefiting society; they developed the road system, so that more people could use more automobiles. Through industrial management they timed labor to the speed of machines. Through the application of inventions they steadily displaced labor with machines. Yet few engineers have been aware of the new problems created by the productive devices which they so skillfully and confidently perfected.

Technological unemployment is only one by-product of the engineer's genius — one, however, from which he himself suffers. For when unemployment became general, engineers were laid off along with others. Ironically, now, the government calls on the jobless engineer to apply his knowledge to putting the other jobless to work. In the process the engineer is learning that many of the time-honored practices of private employment must be discarded. For example, to use labor profitably in private industry one reduces the cost of it by speeding up the work, by dividing and simplifying processes, or by transferring human labor to machines. These are not the methods of public work.

In the public service the engineer must find ways, not to eliminate labor, but to use it lest it be wasted. He can still aim at efficiency and low unit costs in the production of goods, utilities or services, but his first responsibility is to human needs and wants. He is no longer producing goods and services to make profits, but to make jobs. Instead of discharging the worker who cannot keep up, or the worker who does not learn quickly, he must somehow adapt the work and the program to the people for whom it is designed. Or, failing that, he must find other work for the unadaptable workers to do. In his new role the engineer works with people for the public good, striving always to engage them on efficient and useful projects. His is now a problem in human engineering.

THE USE OF EXPERTS HAS JUST BEGUN

Of the many engineers and social workers brought into the public service, there will always be some who will leave it because they have not been able to adapt themselves. Not a few of the social workers have already returned to private agencies, but they are not happy there. Even the private charities have had to adjust themselves to changing conditions; they must find new services to render and new ways of rendering them.

For the government welfare program is not diminishing. It will use more social workers, not only in the expansion of the Social Security Board, but in the many other fields of federal welfare. This is precisely what the most progressive social workers have hoped for.

Of the many engineers brought into the public work relief program, some will go back to private enterprise because they can make more money; others will leave because they have neither the ability nor the desire to cope with human problems. Most of the engineers brought into the public service have found in the necessity for humanizing work a new challenge, and they are accepting it with the same professional integrity that they formerly exhibited in private employment.

Engineers, like social workers, will be needed as long as there is unemployment relief. Viewed logically, the government's Works Program represents the next step in the evolution of the profession, since it returns engineering to the field of public service whence it originally came.

In less than a century, the engineers, working with the theoretical scientists, have produced this complex and chaotic civilization. Now, having built the factories, the engineers face the problem of helping the government spread the advantages of factory production to all the people. With their aid, private industry, through technological improvements, enforced idleness on millions of workers. Now as public servants, the engineers must find ways of turning the idleness into useful and productive channels. The same technical minds that revolutionized the building industry will now have to work out plans to get the people decently and economically housed. They have found ways of transferring from the home to the factory the drudgery of making clothing and processing foods. It now remains for them to help devise the means of returning the benefits of mass production from the factory to the home.

Throughout this experiment in human rehabilitation our vocabulary with reference to relief, public work, and unemployment has been rapidly changing. Among social workers we hear less about the unemployed as "clients," and more about them as "workers." We read less in the newspapers about charity and the dole, and more about work. Very little is said any more about the pauper's oath, and though there was once considerable agitation carried on by associations of taxpayers for disfranchising the "reliefers," today this movement has been effectively checked.

"CERTIFIED" FOR WORK

The principle that government benefits must be democratically distributed among those qualified to receive them applies to relief benefits as much as to the benefits of police protection, the mail service, or free education.

The responsibility for deciding which of the many unemployed workers will get the limited number of jobs to be distributed through the emergency program is a problem of social work. Whether by lot or by rotation from waiting lists, an equitable method of selection must be devised. Thus far the government has recognized need, determined through social investigation, as the basis for granting relief benefits.

Once the workers have been selected or "certified" for work, the next step is to assign them to the work they can do, or to find work they are fitted for. This, in the federal program, is called the "assignment procedure." It is in part a social service function and in part an engineering function, but it involves a new phase of public work administration, a phase which is called "labor relations."

If a worker cannot get along with the foreman, the adjustment of the difficulty may be effected through social work or through engineering, but it also tends to be a special function, related to, but distinct from both. The same problem arises whenever workers are not satisfied with the wages they get, the number of hours they work, or the conditions under which they labor. These matters are related to, but somewhat outside the field of either social work or engineering. Workers on public projects may complain that they are being discriminated against because they are of a different political, religious, or racial group from that of the officials in charge. Surely if workers are discriminated against on any grounds whatsoever, they have a right to speak out and get redress. To handle such problems as these is the function of the labor relations advisor or officer.

On the other hand, while some workers complain of discrimination, others demand preferences. For example, if skilled workers in the building trades insist that every public building project in a city be done by union labor, all needy qualified workers will be excluded because they cannot afford to join a union. Some groups demand preference on the basis of military service, others because they are local residents or natives of the state, or because they have always voted for the political party in power. To grant a preference to any group is to impose a discrimination on another. The task of maintaining a proper balance between them lies within the field of labor relations.

Workers have a right to organize, yet no matter how often that right is acknowledged there is still opposition to it. Public officials are often intolerant toward collective activity on the part of the unemployed. Craft unions in one community, and industrial unions in another, may object if the benefits of a work program go to their rivals. Again, the regular unions may join forces to limit the benefits that might be granted the unions of the unemployed. Therefore, since the public work program cannot play favorites, it is a labor relations function to see that the benefits are equitably distributed.

Employers may oppose the work program, claiming that it pays wages that are too high or that it causes a shortage of labor. Yet if we concede that workers have rights which the government is obliged to respect, we must grant employers their rights, too. This, again, is a labor relations responsibility.

The labor relations official needs to be a person of wide personal contacts, with a liking for people; in short, he must have many of the attributes of a politician. But whereas the politician may honestly support any cause, the labor relations official can have no cause; if he has any bias it must be toward fairness. All public officials should be straightforward, but the labor relations officer must be conspicuously so, and he must be free as well of any suspicion of prejudice or partiality.

THE USE OF EXPERTS

Largely through the aid of social workers, engineers, labor specialists, and experts in other fields, the people as a whole are acquiring a new appreciation of public service. These professionals have added dignity and prestige to the emergency relief work of the federal government. Through their millions of contacts with people, they have succeeded in arousing a national consciousness of pressing social problems that have been long unrecognized.

We were aware of old age dependency, but we never realized the appalling extent or the pitiable effects of it until old people by the thousand began to gather at the federal relief offices. In the same way the entire nation has become aware of the need of young people for work experience and training. This awareness has encouraged the continuation of such agencies as the CCC and NYA.

For many years agricultural workers have suffered from acute malnutrition. A few people have been aware of their plight, but it was never publicly recognized. Today everyone knows about the sharecroppers; the federal program brought their problem out into the open. And now various groups, some newly organized, are putting pressure on the government to relieve the extreme and dangerous poverty that exists in certain rural areas.

For years we have managed somehow to get along despite our chronic social ills, but once the government has brought them to light, we cannot, in good conscience, let them fade out of public consciousness unremedied.

The government is assuming many new burdens that need to be assumed, and, although beset by many handicaps, is attempting to do it professionally. With this acceptance of responsibility has come an increasing demand for experts in the public service. Anything less than the professional approach to these problems could not withstand the scrutiny of critics within the government, nor of those outside among the editors and politicians of the party that is not in power. The integrity of any government is safeguarded by a permanent civil service and a professional-minded personnel.

XI. MANAGEMENT PHASES OF
WORK RELIEF

A WORKING PARTNERSHIP

If a thousand jobless workers in a community are to be employed on public projects, the problem is, first, to ascertain the type of work they can do and then to apply it to work the community would like to have done. This constitutes a radical departure from the old practices of public work; it puts government in partnership with the community in providing work to employ people. Together, the local and federal public agencies plan the projects, buy the materials, supervise the jobs and pay the workers.

Among the arguments used against this method by advocates of big projects is the claim that public work planned and supervised by federal agencies cannot be efficient. Unfortunately for them, the facts do not confirm this charge. It has been amply demonstrated that government engineers can do big jobs more efficiently, at lower cost, and with greater safety than can private contractors. We have proved that relief work projects, when well supervised, are no less efficient than private work. Public work under government auspices need lack nothing in integrity.

This is the more significant when one considers the handicaps under which the government operates. For, in addition to the limitations imposed by the available funds and by the choice of projects suitable to the labor supply, there is the necessity for adjusting the amount of work to changing market requirements. Public work to relieve unemployment should not be booming when private industry is taking on workers. That is one of the dangers of expending too much public money on big long-time projects.

The consequences of overconcentration on big projects was well illustrated in a western state where two large flood control projects sponsored by one federal agency, were competing with each other and with a third large project by another federal agency in the same locality. All three projects were needed, but it was not imperative that all be done at the same time. What happened was that as these projects got under way it was soon discovered that there was not enough relief labor available. The workers were going into private employment.

Similar situations have developed on big public building projects that began at a time when labor was available, but later were handicapped when a private building boom created a shortage of skilled labor. A middle western state, as part of its work relief program, undertook to build about fifty armories. Other projects might perhaps have been more worthwhile, but this state wanted armories, and with so many of them in work it was not long before a shortage of skilled labor developed. The situation was finally met by using fewer skilled workers and a large number of apprentices or helpers. The craft unions, of course, objected. But solely as a by-product of poor planning, a number of youths got a much-needed opportunity to learn something about bricklaying and the stonemason's craft.

Public work for the unemployed is still in an experimental stage. It requires much more imagination and more careful planning than the promotion of big expensive projects. Most important of all, such a program must be extremely adaptable; if it is not, it will be wasteful. It can be successful only if there is the maximum of cooperation between the federal government as the provider of money and guidance, and the local communities as sponsors and administrators. Without comprehensive local responsibility and federal responsiveness to local needs, the welfare phase of the unemployment program could not be realized.

ENCROACHING ON ONE ANOTHER

Up to now, the sole purpose of emergency public work for the unemployed has been to preserve the existing economic order and to restore the capitalist industrial system to its idealized equilibrium. Whether that can be done remains to be seen.

If private industrial enterprise were ideally operated, jobs would be available for all workers and opportunities for advancement would never run short. Private employment failing, should the government assume responsibility for giving work to all those who cannot get private jobs? The government, by refusing to go that far, has created a nice problem in management — that of giving some work to as many unemployed persons as possible.

Although the aim of the federal work program is to function outside the field of private enterprise, it is impossible to employ two or three million workers on public jobs without to some extent disturbing private employment; the two systems, public and private, cannot exist side by side without encroaching on one another. Theoretically, the system of private work has the right of way, and the system of emergency public work is expected to fit in as well as it can; as the first picks up, the second is supposed to decline. But if the first system, that of private employment, does not pick up as it should, what then should be the policy of the government in maintaining the system of public work?

The task of the federal agencies in charge of work relief is at the same time to respect the purposes of the government, the rights of industry, and the needs of the unemployed. In other words, there should be no invasions of industry's rights that can possibly be avoided. There must, however, be some. The invasions will be one, or both, of two types. If the government pays more than prevailing rates on public work, it may invade the rights of certain marginal low-paying employers who have set prevailing rates at levels which do not attract the workers. A second type of invasion is typified by public work projects that are competitive in nature.

INVASION — NOT BY INTENT

Work for the unemployed would be utterly without justification if it did not relieve pressure in the overstocked labor market, and, were it not useful work, it could not be done with integrity. Thus work relief may invade not only industrial territory, but also, and to a greater extent, governmental tradition and equilibrium in states, counties, and municipalities. These are invasions, not by intent, but in effect.

Federal public work for the unemployed is not designed to invade the domain of local government. It is intended simply to assist localities with programs that they would normally be expected to carry out themselves. Such an emergency program must enjoy considerable latitude to meet local needs from one community to another. Failure to meet the need for funds in one town might cause the unemployed untold hardship. In another, failure to fit the job-providing program to local resources might result in doing for a community what it could and should do for itself. This, in turn, might impose another kind of injury by discouraging local initiative and financial responsibility.

In still another sense a work-giving program must be flexible. It must be able to meet local emergency needs such as flood, drought, fire, or crop failure. These have never been the responsibility of public work agencies established to finance and supervise big jobs.

We have already observed during recent floods how the work force of such agencies as WPA and CCC can be organized instantaneously into mobile units. These workers, because they can be shifted from their regular work to disaster spots, constitute a standing army prepared to meet all emergencies.

A work program, to be efficiently and realistically operated, must have access to necessary current information. That was imperative in managing the federal cattle program, the drought program, and the fight against the Ohio River flood.

If facts are needed, it is the responsibility of the localities to supply them; not any facts gathered in any way, but the essential information prepared so that it can be used. The federal government, having written the specifications, must depend upon the cooperation of the individual communities, or the work could not be properly accomplished. It means the loss of some local autonomy, but any other arrangement for carrying out the unemployment program would result only in waste and lost motion.

Unavoidably in public work the responsibility for financial control tends to concentrate in federal hands. Government agencies have to render scrupulous accounts through uniform reporting methods, and no allowances for local practices and local differences can be made in counting or accounting for the funds. In some communities this is regarded as an invasion of local control, because the federal government does not leave the counting and spending of its money to local public officials.

But financial responsibility for public work must be centralized if payrolls and record-keeping are not to become hopelessly confused. It is only supervisory responsibility for public work that cannot be centralized efficiently. The test of good administration is the maximum of local supervision that exists in any community.

Insistence on local responsibility for planning a project, for reporting the unemployment needs, and for getting a project under way, is the best means of stimulating local interest in the quality of the work. Experience has proved that local supervisory officials on a work program lose nothing of their integrity by being paid from federal funds, so long as they work in the interest of the local community. If the project is sound, the quality of the work high, and the maximum amount of wages distributed among the relief workers, both federal and local interests have been well served.

WORK RELIEF MUST BE FLEXIBLE

Whatever the number of workers employed in a federal program, the chief administrative problem is the equitable distribution of the jobs among regions, states, and localities. For example, if WPA had money enough to employ 1,500,000 workers during any given month, how should the jobs be allocated? How many should go to the New England states, the southern states or to the Middle West? How many jobs should be given to New York as compared with Ohio, Kentucky, or Arizona? And when the jobs have been allocated to the states, how should they be distributed within states? What portion of the California quota should be given to Los Angeles or to San Francisco?

Determining factors in such decisions change with every season and with changing conditions in the private labor market. Federal and state WPA officials, to make these allocations fairly, must have before them a continuous flow of factual information, and they must have it at least a month or two in advance.

Failure to realize approximate equality in the distribution of quotas to states and localities would have most unfortunate results. Too many jobs would antagonize employers; too few would impose hardships on the unemployed. Cutting the quota too soon would injure the workers; not to cut the quotas soon enough might hamper the employers. This problem of timing, concerns most the planting and harvesting of agricultural crops, including cotton, garden truck, fruits, and sugar beets; but it also applies to the fishing, lumber, and pulp industries.

It would be unfair to release beet field workers from public jobs at the end of February or early in March if they were not needed until early in April. It would be equally unfair to release workers from public jobs at all if they have had no experience in the beet fields. The entire procedure also involves the rates of pay in beet fields, and the effect on those rates if no workers, or if too many, are released.

A work program must therefore be adaptable to changing employment needs in any community. But it must also be intelligently responsive to local social needs. It is obvious that social needs are served best when the unemployed are assigned to work they are fitted to do. If able-bodied workers are entitled to employment at all, they deserve to get work that is suited to their training, experience, and strength, provided, of course, that such work can be reasonably provided.

ILL-HOUSED, ILL-CLAD, ILL-FED

If the proper variety of work cannot be provided to utilize the skills of the unemployed, related or similar work should be made available to them. And if the private labor market no longer demands the skills possessed by certain workers, the relief program must explore the possibilities of teaching them other skills. In the case of workers who have had no training or work experience, the solution lies in training. These are the social needs of the unemployed which competitive industry cannot adequately meet, and which government cannot ignore. They are too diverse to be satisfied on a national scale, and hence must be approached in terms of state and local situations in cooperation with the federal agencies.

Quite apart from the needs of all the jobless, a work program must consider the needs of certain special groups. Among these are the Negroes, disadvantaged in the labor market in numbers far out of proportion to their percentage in the general population. Another group comprises the employable women with no work experience in private industry, and a third embraces the older workers.

All over the country there is a growing demand for old age pensions, paralleled by a movement to retire workers, usually at the age of sixty-five. Rarely are these pensions adequate and rarely do the workers willingly accept them. They call forced retirement discrimination and demand work, even if their wages are no more than the pension. To force such aging workers into publicly supported idleness is to give federal approval to the unsound economy of scarcity. Not to use their labor is economically wasteful. When the local communities are unable, or unwilling, to make provision for these disadvantaged groups, it becomes the function of government to protect their interests.

Unemployment among youth is one of the most serious administrative problems that confronts the work program. From the point of view of the community it may prove to be more important to provide work for youths than for adults. Yet by one means or another, young men and women find themselves excluded from relief work. Temporary employment is given to some of them, but too often these assignments are only meaningless substitutes for work. They are never popular with young people who want real work and are being demoralized for lack of it.

The New Deal Administration has admitted that one-third of the people·are ill-housed, ill-clad, and ill-fed, and has promised that something will be done about it. Something is being done about it through public work relief, but not enough. If more people are to be put to work, more work has to be found for them and new ways of using their labor must be devised. It is not a sound policy to use most men workers on road jobs or most women workers in sewing rooms. If a third of the people are to be better housed, the government may have to assign the unemployed to building new houses or improving the old ones.

If a third of the nation is ill-clad, and if something is to be done about it, the government may have to alter the existing restrictions against making clothing, bedding, and furnishings for the unemployed. With so much labor available, there is no reason for anyone's being ill-housed, ill-clad, or ill-fed. Actually, it is the labor of these ill-cared for people that is being wasted. To meet this situation a drastic revision of our present work policy may be necessary.

PREVAILING WAGES

On regular old style public work done by contractors, both federal and state governments maintain a policy of paying prevailing wages. Normally, the prevailing wage is the local hourly rate for any given occupation. If in one locality several rates are being paid for the same occupation, the prevailing wage may be determined by taking the weighted average of all the rates or the rate which is paid to the largest number of workers.

Work relief agencies, principally WPA, started out to pay what is called a "security wage," which is really a monthly payment based on three conditioning factors:

1. On the basis of geographical location. Originally the states were grouped in four regions but now there are only three. The lower rates prevail in the southern states.

2. On the basis of urbanization. The counties in each state are divided into five classes, depending on the size of the largest city in the county. Cities are classes from those under 5,000 to those over 100,000.

3. On the basis of occupational classification. The occupations and skills are classed as unskilled, intermediate, skilled, professional, and technical.

Organized labor protested that the security wage was an invasion of the prevailing wage principle. Skilled workers warned that their rates in private industry were in jeopardy. Finally, after a great deal of pressure, the method of wage payment was changed.

A skilled worker in a large industrial city no longer works 140 hours a month for $85; he works out the $85 at the prevailing wage. Thus if the hourly rate for his craft is $1.25, he is required to work 68 hours. The same holds for other occupations, although in low wage states, the rate for unskilled labor — especially for women — is usually in excess of prevailing hourly wages.

All security workers now receive a monthly payment ranging from $21 for unskilled labor in the rural South to $94 for professional and technical workers in the large cities of the northern states.

The security monthly wage, paid on the basis of hourly rates, has had certain unforeseen consequences. For example:

1. Certain types of workers get assignments to work agencies such as

WPA and settle down as if project employment were a regular occupation. Some fear to take other jobs because they have no assurance that they can get back on WPA if their outside work stops.

2. Among the skilled and technical workers on WPA are many who have ability but do not have speed. At the prevailing rates of pay for first-class workers they cannot be profitably employed by private industry. Yet these workers on WPA get a prevailing rate for less than prevailing amounts of work. Perhaps they should have the monthly security payments for their classifications, but should be required to do more hours per month to equal the output of a first-class worker.

3. For efficient skilled or technical workers, the present security and prevailing rate policy is a temptation to seek outside employment after the monthly work requirements on project employment have been met. A skilled worker receiving in New York City $85 per month at a prevailing rate of $1.50 per hour, earns his payments in a work month of about 56 hours. The rest of the month is his. The temptation is present to secure supplementary work, which too frequently may be at rates of pay less than the prevailing wage.

It is good public policy in areas of extremely low living standards to allow project employment to pay slightly in excess of prevailing wages. In a rural county of the south the WPA rate of $21 for 140 hours of work is about double the wage for the same amount of labor on a farm. It would be twice the farm rate even on the basis of an hourly wage.

Under quite opposite circumstances, it may not be good public policy to pay the prevailing hourly rate or better. In high wage areas it puts relief work in competition with private employment. Furthermore, it tends to place the workers who have security jobs in a preferred class as compared with other unemployed workers excluded from these jobs because of quota limitations.

SAFETY AND MORALE

Between one and two million workers are employed every day on emergency jobs provided by the federal government. Every type of hazard is present in the various conditions under which this jobless army earns a living. To care for the well-being of such a host of toilers is probably the world's biggest safety job, and the most difficult.

On WPA projects more than on others, workers of every type, with training and without, are brought together. The government may not operate factories, mines, or transportation lines, yet workers from these industries are among the jobless of every community. They have to be put to work in the ditch or on the roads. They are taught to use tools — shovels, picks, axes, saws — and many do not learn with ease. Women who never worked before are put at machines in sewing rooms. Young workers who have never learned to "team up" with fellow workers or to "square off" to work are assigned to project crews.

To bring together so many workers of so many kinds, and to employ them so that the awkwardness of some does not endanger others is a challenge to administration. It is necessary to segregate those who cannot work on high places, or in a deep ditch, as well as those who cannot, for their own safety, be assigned to heavy work.

When the Works Program got under way in 1935 special provision was made to protect all security wage workers through the federal compensation service. Safety sections were established as a regular part of all operations, and something of the success of the plan is indicated in the figures for WPA. It was possible, on the basis of industrial experience in similar types of work, to estimate what the accident and fatality rate on WPA might be.

During the first two years of WPA, ending June, 1937, the total number of persons on all projects worked approximately five and a half billion man-hours.

For that many billion man-hours of labor, according to estimates posted in advance, 1,650 fatalities were expected, or one death for each 3,300,000 man-hours worked. The actual number of fatalities was 814, equivalent to one death for each 6,540,000 man-hours worked.

On the basis of the same estimates, there should have been 213,-000 lost-time injuries in the course of five and a half billion manhours of work. The actual number of lost-time injuries was 95,000.

The excellence of that record may be explained by the fact that between states and within states there is keen rivalry on WPA for the safety record. Recently, when the Wisconsin WPA finished six months without a fatality, the good news was wired to Washington and neighboring states. WPA safety engineers, despite obstacles not often found in private employment, are setting a safety record which will be hard for industry to touch.

Nothing need be said here to justify the safety motive in any type of work. Safety is good business; lost-time injuries and fatalities cost money. But on relief work there is another reason why a good safety record is worth striving for. It is well known that the higher the morale of the workers, the better is the safety record. In like manner, as the safety record of WPA has improved, so in turn has the morale.

The value of high morale on work relief projects cannot be overemphasized. It must be remembered that a great many of the unemployed had reached the verge of physical and spiritual disintegration, and that work relief has been an effort to restore to them their well-being and self-respect. Whether the effort has been successful, and in large part it has been, at least the objective is defensible.

On the part of the government, WPA makes it clear that project employment is temporary support until workers can get private employment; that the jobs will be given and may be held without discrimination, and that complaints will be heard and adjusted so far as the limitations of the program permit.

On the part of the workers, WPA expects a fair day's work, a conscientious effort to find private employment and cooperation in helping the program serve the community. If by these or other incentives, WPA succeeds in raising the morale of workers disemployed by industry, the social effects will be well worth the cost of the program.

THE. MEANS TEST

Eligible workers are certified, as we have noted, on the basis of a social investigation to determine their need. This method, called the "means test," is not popular with the unemployed, who call it the "pauper's oath."

Sentiment to abolish the means test is on the increase, yet a considerable section of public opinion still favors such a test. Its sponsors look approvingly on it as a safeguard against the possibility of too many workers seeking public aid. They believe the means test has certain moral values. But so many millions of families and individuals have already applied for relief or work relief that the means test has been robbed of its sting and whatever moral values it may have had have about vanished.

If the means test were to be abandoned as the basis for selecting unemployed workers, the next likely method would be to select them, according to their classifications, from waiting lists. There is actually no reason for believing that selection from a waiting list would lead to any more abuses than does case work certification. It is not necessary and may, in fact, be harmful to retain the means test, which, like the pauper's oath, is one of those outmoded devices intended to humiliate the poor.

Basically, the objective of the employment program is to help workers until they can help themselves get established in normal employment. This purpose is a distinctly social one and its implications are more far-reaching than merely giving work, although work is a means to a social end. But when social objectives are introduced into a program for providing jobs, the way is opened for other considerations which are also social.

From the viewpoint of the economy as a whole, unemployed persons are given jobs in order that they may go on buying and consuming as workers normally do. Thus, for performing useful work the unemployed are given money with which to buy goods to make work for others. The entire process is called rehabilitation.

The possibilities of rehabilitation for different types of workers vary widely in different situations, as do the rehabilitation possibilities for individuals. In this respect, what should the unemployed workers expect of the government and what are the responsibilities of government to the unemployed?

The answer to both questions depends upon the workers involved. Young men and women have a right to jobs and training. If industry cannot or will not recognize that right, they must look to the government. And what of the various types of marginal workers, especially those being crowded out of the competitive labor market?

Whatever the needs of the unemployed may be, the public work program cannot deal with them adequately except at close range. It must work out a cooperative relationship with other public agencies, with private agencies and with industry in serving the unemployed.

It is this social responsibility toward the disadvantaged groups in our society that makes the work program for the jobless different from other forms of public work. In assuming this social responsibility, the government has aroused concern in certain quarters about the security of capitalism. Such fears are entirely unwarranted. As a matter of sober fact, alarmists should realize that such steps as the government has taken to relieve dire need are the best possible insurance against more drastic changes in the existing economic order.

INDEX

Agricultural Adjustment Administration, 13; purpose of, 12
American Federation of Labor, 115, 120; unemployment estimate of, 31
American Guide, The, 67
American Roadbuilders Assn., 111
America's Capacity to Consume, 54
Army Engineering Corps, 49
Army of the Commonwealth, 4
Associated General Contractors of America, 111

Balancing the budget, 70, 71
Bear Mountain Park, 50
Biggers, John D., 32
"Boondoggling," 14, 22, 62, 65–67
Brookings Institution, 54, 55
Brown University, 30
Buildings, construction of public and private, 46, 60, 63, 136

Census, of unemployed, 31–37, 39; United States, 36
Civil Works Administration, 15, 16, 18, 123, 125; cost of, 24, 25; discontinued, 16; features of, 15; methods of, 16
Civilian Conservation Corps, 10, 49, 59, 101, 102, 134, 138; cost of, 24; employment figures, 21, 32; purpose of, 9; standing force of, 9
Cleveland, President, 4
Committee for Industrial Organization, 115, 120
Committee on the Cost of Medical Care, 47, 51
Coxey, General Jacob, 4

Death rate, 53

Education, 53; expenditure for, 54
Emergency Relief and Reconstruction Act, 8, 9
Emergency Relief Appropriation Act of 1937, 37, 110
Emergency Relief Bureau of New York City, 50
Engineers, 129–132, 134

Farm Security Administration, 47
Federal Administration of Public Works (*see* Public Works Administration)
Federal Arts Project, 66
Federal Emergency Relief Act of 1933, 10
Federal Emergency Relief Administration, 10, 11, 13–15, 18, 19, 56, 111–113, 123, 124, 126, 128; cost of, 24, 25; education project, 54; program, 16, 17; purpose of, 10; statistics, 21, 22; wages, 80; Work Division, 16, 17
Federal Relief (*see* Relief)

149

Fellows, Perry A., 99
Forestry Service, 49, 59

Government Printing Office, 59
Greenbelt, a housing development, 47

Health education, 51, 52
Hoover, Herbert, 76; and recovery, 7, 8; conferences with industrialists, 5
Hospitals, 46, 47; services of, 51–53
Housing, 47, 48

Idleness (*see* Unemployed)
Income, classification in groups, 54, 55; losses in national, 7, 24, 25; national, 6
Industry (*see* Private Industry)

Jackson, Andrew, 124
Jones Beach, 50

Labor market, free, 84–89, 92, 129
Labor relations, 132, 133
Labor unions, 15, 87, 93, 94, 123; as pressure groups, 113; craft, 101, 113, 114, 118, 133, 136; industrial, 133; unemployed, 114–116, 118–121, 123, 133
Landon, Alfred M., 76

Means test, 147
Milbank Memorial Fund, 46

National Industrial Conference Board, 31
National Institute of Health, survey, 52
National Recovery Administration, 12, 13; regulation of labor market, 92, 93
National Survey of Potential Product Capacity, 50, 51
National Unemployed Workers Protective League, 116, 117
National Youth Administration, 134; employment figures, 32
Negroes, 40, 41, 82, 141
New Deal, 10, 11, 68, 94, 111, 120, 122, 125, 142
New York City Housing Authority, 50
New York Sun, unemployment estimate, 31

Old Deal, 10; programs, 11

Pennsylvania Security League, 115, 116
Post Office Department, unemployment census, 32
Pressure groups, 107–110, 113, 115, 116, 118, 120, 121
Private industry, 57–60, 63, 64, 84, 86, 88–92, 94, 97–100, 103, 112, 125, 129, 130, 131, 137

Public highways, 46, 50; cost of, 45
Public Works Administration, 13, 15, 16, 20, 58, 119, 126; contract method, 14; cost of, 24, 25; expenditure for labor and materials, 22, 23; housing program, 47; percentage from relief rolls, 23; purpose of, 12; statistics, 21, 22

Railroad crossings, 46
Reconstruction Finance Corporation, 3, 11, 126; purposes of, 9
Recreational facilities, 50, 51, 67
Relief, 11, 61, 62, 64, 68, 69, 75, 78, 84, 88, 90, 95, 97, 99, 115, 131, 132, 147; administering unemployment, 11, 107; administrative forces, 18; appropriation for, 71; benefits for women, 38, 39; benefits for young and old, 39; burden of, 109, 110; CCC as pioneer agency of, 10; cost of, 24, 25, 74, 80; discrimination in, 40, 41; distribution of work, 140; elimination through unions, 94; federal and work, 3, 17, 18, 19, 109, 111, 113, 134, 135, 142; for agricultural workers, 82, 83; form of work, 14; illness among families, 52; loans, 9; moral implications of, 108, 110; philosophy of, 19; program, 10, 13, 18, 23, 55, 72, 85, 91, 99, 102, 114, 122, 123, 125, 127, 137, 138, 139; safety on, 146; standards, 17; statistics, 22; test of public, 59, 60; training by agencies, 101; workers on, 35, 103, 104
Resettlement Administration, cost of, 24; housing program, 47
Roosevelt, administration, 8, 71; assumes office, 9

Sanitation, 49, 50
Smoot-Hawley tariff of 1930, 5
Social Security, 38, 103, 130
Social workers, 126–132, 134
Society for the Advancement of Management, 99
Soil Erosion, service, 49
Supreme Court, declares NRA and AAA unconstitutional, 12

Teachers, 54, 66

Unemployed (and Unemployment), 3, 7, 8, 10, 14, 15, 17, 19, 20, 23–25, 31, 36, 39, 45, 68, 69, 72–75, 79, 81, 85–87, 90, 92, 95, 99, 103, 104, 108, 112–114, 127–130, 132, 136–138, 140, 141, 147; administering relief to, 11; among youth, 142; "Army of Commonwealth," 4; census of, 31–35, 37, 39; cost of, 6, 7, 24, 76, 80; crafts and skills of, 98; foreign born, 110; in 1840, 30; increase of, 9; learning to employ, 13; on flood and erosion control projects, 49; patriotism of, 111; rehabilitation of, 105, 131, 147, 148; seasons, 44, 84; security for, 91; skilled and unskilled, 41, 42, 88, 89; statistics, 6; unions of, 114–116, 118–121, 123, 133; women, 37–39, 56, 141; work for, 78; work needs of, 59
Unions (see Labor Unions)
United States Employment Service, 20, 36, 37, 85, 88; jobs for women, 37, 38; unemployment report, 32, 34, 35, 39
United States Office of Education, reports, 53, 54
United States Public Health Service, 52

Veterans of Industry of America, 115

Wages and hours, 21, 80, 89, 90, 92, 113, 132, 143, 144
Wagner Housing Act, 48
Water Control, 48–50, 136
Wayland, Francis, 30, 31, 98
Welfare Bureau, 58
Women, unemployed, 37–39, 56, 141
"Women's Brigade," 37
Work Relief (*see* Relief)
Workers Alliance, 115, 116, 120; "Women's Brigade," 37
Works Program, 18, 20, 41, 64, 113, 124, 126, 128, 131, 145; employment figures, 21, 35; general objective and basic principles, 19; method of administering relief, 20
Works Progress Administration, 17, 19, 36, 38, 51, 58, 59, 61, 62, 64, 82–85, 89, 93, 95–97, 99, 101–103, 109–111, 113, 116, 117, 119, 122–124, 126, 128, 138, 140, 143–145; classification, 42; cost of, 24, 25; Defense Council, 117; education projects, 54; employment figures, 32, 35; expenditures for labor and materials, 22, 23; fatalities on, 145, 146; percentage from relief rolls, 23; statistics, 21, 22; wages and hours under, 21, 80, 144
"World Unemployment Day," 115